Filled with powerful affirmations, meditations,
and exercises, this wise and practical book is designed to help you:

- reveal your true self—your most precious gift to others
- consciously design the relationships you most want
- open yourself to partnering with God
- discover the power of unreasonable giving
- achieve intimacy by speaking from your heart
- heal the hurt in difficult relationships
- awaken love through simple daily acts

Real love is the greatest purpose of our lives. Let Mary Manin
Morrissey help you discover it.

"Mary is one of our most powerful and enlightened teachers."
—Wayne W. Dyer, author of *Manifest Your Destiny*

NO LESS THAN GREATNESS

GREATNESS

The Seven Spiritual Principles That Make Real Love Possible

MARY MANIN MORRISSEY

BANTAM BOOKS
NEW YORK TORONTO LONDON SYDNEY AUCKLAND

NO LESS THAN GREATNESS

A Bantam Book

PUBLISHING HISTORY
Bantam hardcover edition published August 2001
Bantam trade paperback edition / September 2002

Library of Congress Catalog Card Number: 2001025784.

ISBN: 0-553-37903-8

Published simultaneously in the United States and Canada

Bantam Books are published by Bantam Books, a division of
Random House, Inc. Its trademark, consisting of the words
"Bantam Books" and the portrayal of a rooster, is Registered
in U.S. Patent and Trademark Office and in other countries.
Marca Registrada. Bantam Books, 1540 Broadway, New
York, New York 10036.

PRINTED IN THE UNITED STATES OF AMERICA

BVG   10   9   8   7   6   5   4   3   2   1

I lovingly dedicate this book to my parents,

Jack and Dorothy Manin,

who steadfastly believe in the seed of greatness and nurture its growth through their consistent and unconditional love.

CONTENTS

THE POWER OF UNREASONABLE GIVING

FLUENT IN THE LANGUAGE OF THE HEART

TRANSFORMING DIFFICULT RELATIONSHIPS

CELEBRATING EACH DAY

NO LESS THAN
GREATNESS

INTRODUCTION:
A DIVINE ASSIGNMENT

Growing up, my youngest son fully expected to become a movie star. My daughter wanted to be a prima ballerina on Broadway. My friend Ginger wanted to be a famous artist. As children, we instinctively know that we are destined for greatness.

Life doesn't always turn out the way we expected. Somewhere along the line, most of us realize that only a favored few are ever going to walk on the moon. Then disillusionment sets in. We can't have the greatness we thought was our birthright, so we wind up settling for far less instead.

But settling is not what we're meant for. As kids, we had it right: God endows us with the potential to live a great life, because greatness really is our destiny. The way we find greatness isn't by winning an Oscar. We fulfill our desire for greatness in learning to fulfill our basic nature as children of God, from whom we have inherited a tremendous capacity for love. In learning to love well through every relationship that we have, we touch greatness beyond anything the world honors and offers.

Each of us has a divine assignment: to live in and express love. It is a task you are uniquely equipped to perform. Nobody else will ever know the exact mix of people that you do. Nobody else will ever have the opportunities you do to bless their lives. You have been designated to leave a loving impression on your partner, parents, children, neighbors, coworkers and a whole host of people you have yet to encounter. Some of these people will seem to irritate and interrupt your life. They will invite your blood pressure to rise. Yet this unique set of individuals, whose only commonality is you, has been placed in your path for a reason. When you increase the presence of love in their lives, they can in turn accomplish and contribute in ways you could never fathom. Like George Bailey in *It's a Wonderful Life*, you cannot begin to imagine how your loving influence can shape the world. Seeded in every one of us is a desire to make a difference; we don't want to live and die without having left our mark.

Learning to live in love is life's greatest lesson, and our daily life is the curriculum. But how do we do it? From personal experience, I know that nothing can bring more joy than relationships and nothing can break our hearts like the very same thing: relationships. We deeply desire the good but often don't give much thought to how we relate to others until trouble sets in.

Learning to live in love is life's greatest lesson, and our daily life is the curriculum.

Take, for example, a study I read in which several families were videotaped so that researchers could tally how people tend to communicate with one another.

Can you guess the most oft-uttered phrases? They weren't "How are you?" or "I love you." No, the words husbands and wives, brothers and sisters spoke more often than any other were "What's on?" and "Move."

It's easy to laugh, but even the most seemingly blissful

beginning can wind up more predictable than a television rerun. We all desire great relationships but often settle for just getting by. Many of us have stopped questioning the fact that we may know fictitious TV families more intimately than we do our own.

The good news is, by following the spiritual principles outlined in this book, our most meaningful conversations don't have to be about the remote. We are created for something far greater and wider reaching. We are meant to learn a love that overcomes all challenges, difficulty and estrangement. Our task is not to try to get that love into us, because unconditional, dynamic love is already here. Our task is to uncover it, to touch and experience it, and then to express this dynamic love in such a way that we fulfill the purpose for which we were born.

But we cannot do it alone—nor are we meant to.

Our education teaches facts and figures and how to successfully negotiate most of the turns in life. But it doesn't teach us how to navigate and nurture deeply fulfilling relationships. So when our relationships falter, we may turn to shelves of self-help books that tell us how to fight fair or communicate better or manage a difficult child.

"Self-help"—as if we could possibly do it alone! What most of these books don't tell us is that relationship with a Higher Power lies at the core of our ability to truly find and live in love.

~~~~~~~~~

Relationship with a Higher Power lies at the core of our ability to truly find and live in love.

~~~~~~~~~

When Jesus was asked what the most important thing in this life was, had He answered in a single word, that word would have been "love." He defined love as relationship—not merely as a bond with others, but with ourselves and, most important, with our Creator. Jesus said: "You shall love the Lord your God with all your heart, with all your soul and with all your might. This is the first and great commandment. And the second is like it. You shall love your neighbor as yourself. On these two commandments hang all the Law and the Prophets." (Matthew 22:37–40)

When we feel used up, at the end of our seeming capacity to cope with a spouse or child or friend, we can learn to draw strength from something greater. Our Creator offers the guidance and inspiration to transform our relationships. Our ego and intellect, and especially our patience, have limits. What appears as dark night and tough times will always lead to greater joy as we learn to open to God's guidance, presence and grace.

I know this relationship is available to us, because it has transformed my life. As a young woman, I felt so let down. No relationship had turned out right, marriage in particular. A homecoming princess kicked out of high school for becoming pregnant, I was home changing dirty diapers while my friends were collecting their diplomas.

I'll never forget the day, shortly after the birth of my second child, when I bought a sweater at the mall to cheer myself up. For a moment, I did feel better. In those days, with money so scarce, a new article of clothing was a special treat. Coming out of the department store, I saw a swirl of people around me. They all seemed to be smiling and laughing. Everywhere I turned, happy couples were holding hands. I looked down and saw my own hand grasping the paper handle of a shopping bag, and suddenly my new cotton cardigan felt unbearably heavy. This wasn't what I wanted to be holding. I didn't know what I craved, only that I stood surrounded by throngs of shoppers, lived in a home with healthy children and a loyal husband, and had never felt so alone.

Things got worse. I reached the point of total despair after my husband and I argued horribly one evening. I ran outside into the pouring rain, drenched in hopelessness. With nothing to look forward to, ending my life actually seemed like a pretty good idea. In desperation, I screamed out, "Help me!" and as I did, a phrase planted itself in my mind—"There must be a better way." In that instant, I felt the Presence of something greater than myself. I did not know precisely what had happened, but I sensed caring, and love.

As a child, I had thought of God as a white-bearded fellow up in the sky who either granted wishes on command or punished me when I misbehaved. That relationship, rather than maturing, became strained, even estranged (sort of like my marriage). Now, in the midst of my great loneliness, I sensed a Presence, One who saw me as something more than a young woman whose shameful pregnancy had rendered her unworthy.

**In the midst of my great loneliness,
I sensed a Presence.**

How can I possibly describe such a Presence? It was the difference between being a child left alone in an empty house at night and being a child who knows that her mother is in the next room. Even though she can't see or hear her mother, she feels comforted by her warm, loving, protective presence.

And while a human parent can't always be with us, I sensed that my spiritual Parent would never abandon me. A long-forgotten bit of scripture came flooding back to me: I was *created in the image and likeness of God*. I clung to that phrase like a life raft: *the image and likeness of God*. I'd felt so powerless, so helpless. Maybe I had within me a creativity I didn't even understand. It dawned on me that in some way I'd been creating a miserable marriage. I'd been manufacturing my own loneliness. Maybe I could create something better. With that realization came a feeling: Maybe God wasn't only up in the sky, but present everywhere, including at the very center of me.

I loved my little boys so much—nothing they did could make me love them less. I realized that if I as a human being could feel that way about my children, how much more could God feel for all of us? Regardless of what might lie ahead, I would never be alone again.

After this brief, yet powerful encounter with God, I entered a new phase of my life. I was like a thirsty sponge, soaking up everything I could find on various religions, spirituality, ancient philosophy and mysticism. I took both prayer and meditation classes just to ensure I wouldn't miss any opportunity to get to know the Presence that was making Itself known to me now that I was finally paying attention. I practiced seeing the Presence of God in every person and in the natural world around me, from flowers in bloom to the intense shades of green in the trees. I felt as if I had walked out of a small dark closet and stepped into daylight. Literally, I was discovering a new kind of life.

I wanted friends and family to share my sense of excitement, only to wind up dumbfounded by their lack of interest. My friends began joking, "Mary's got religion," because I was so full of the incredible discovery that I did not have to go through life alone. They yawned or laughed at me. I heaped revelations onto everyone I met, a mother force-feeding strained peas, saying, "They're good for you, really, just try them," instead of allowing the baby to pick up the spoon for herself.

I tried so hard to make myself understood. Once, standing in the kitchen at my parents' house, I rambled on about how I had discovered that God had a personal interest in all of us and could help anyone who was willing. After a few minutes, Dad went into the living room and switched on the football game. Mom put on her apron and was cutting vegetables for a salad, but at least she continued to listen, murmuring and nodding to me in encouragement. Finally she looked up and said, "Honey, let me ask you something . . ."

Relieved that I finally had gotten through, I held my breath in anticipation of her question.

"Honey," she said, "do you want Ranch or Thousand Island?"

Since that time, I've learned to share my good news without hitting people over the head. The presence of God unfolds in our lives gradually, guiding us ever closer to perfect love—the same kind of unjudging love God has for us we can demonstrate for one another. I realize that no matter our behavior, what we all want most isn't to be right, to get revenge or to do better than the next person. What we want most is love. Knowing this, I began to view others with more compassion, including my husband. The years we spent together were a powerful opportunity to learn love. The gift of new perspective was that while he and I were ultimately not meant to spend our entire lives together, we could still love one another and deeply respect one another as parents and former partners. Some people call divorce failure. My experience teaches me to think of our marriage after twenty-six years as completed rather than failed.

The presence of God unfolds in our lives gradually, guiding us ever closer to perfect love—the same kind of unjudging love God has for us we can demonstrate for one another.

We each have the opportunity for a life of greatness and all the people on our path are gifts to help us achieve our purpose. This can be true for you even if you feel embattled and discouraged in your relationship with a difficult parent, spouse, child or friend. This can be true even if you have been so badly hurt that loving again seems unimaginable. This can be true even if you feel you have destroyed your best chance for happiness. It is never too late to discover a way that leads to extraordinary living.

~~~~~~~

What we want most is love.

~~~~~~~

This is not a text to merely read, but a book you *do*. In a restaurant, reading a menu may make you salivate, but it won't satiate your hunger. Similarly, knowing about God doesn't fulfill you in the same way as knowing God. The practices detailed in this book will help lead you to an authentic partnership with your Creator that will transform every other relationship in your life.

~~~~~~~

We each have the opportunity for a life of greatness and all the people on our path are gifts to help us achieve our purpose.

~~~~~~~

We really can find perfect love in imperfect relationships.

What do I mean by this? Deep down, what we want most is not to win the argument. Our goal in life is not to resent someone who has hurt us. Being defensive or judgmental are things that we do, but they are not who we are. We practice perfect love by acknowledging all those very human emotions, but not letting them chart our course.

For example, practicing perfect love means that I want to be the world's most caring, loving mother. But if my son says, "Mom, why don't you ever listen to me? You're always on your cell phone," I've got to pause. Sure, maybe I'll feel defensive. I'll want to say, "Listen, it's because of all the work I do that we can afford your school." But defensiveness won't take me where

I want to go, and that is to be closer to my son, to God and to myself. Practicing perfect love means I'm willing to risk hearing something that I don't want to hear. It's recognizing that even as I feel defensive, I know that I want to learn perfect love better, and my relationship with my son is today's classroom.

So how do we do it? This book will show you how. You will rekindle your natural curiosity, realizing that no matter how well you think you know a loved one, there is still so much to discover. You will tap into your God-given power to design and build precisely the relationships you deeply desire. You will find that love isn't merely a feeling, but an active verb. You will learn to identify the habits that may be keeping others at a distance. And yes, you will recognize those times you are stuck in a pattern I call "sleeping with frogs," and how to get free.

The people in the following chapters have embraced family after decades of bare tolerance, rebuilt marital trust after the worst kind of betrayal. They have found partners, rediscovered their own partners and forged bonds with their children they never thought possible. They really know what it means to wake up each morning feeling "It doesn't get much better than this."

Every chapter ends with a practical spiritual practice that you can put to work in your everyday life. For more than a quarter of a century, I have been honing these practices. They have transformed the relationships in my life and in the lives of thousands of others. Through these practices, you will discover what Jesus described as "the pearl of great price," a Presence so precious that there is no material object you would not sacrifice to touch this experience.

Remember the child's truth: You are going to be someone when you grow up. True greatness doesn't come from fame or money. True greatness comes from finding and living in perfect love. You are a child of God, and with God, there is nothing beyond your capacity to create.

DO I HAVE WHAT IT TAKES?

SPIRITUAL PRINCIPLE

Who you really are is a child of God. Nothing is missing; there is only much to be revealed.

My business is not to remake myself,
But to make the absolute best of what God
made.

—ROBERT BROWNING

1. A Case of Mistaken Identity

At first, I was reluctant to show Michael my engagement ring. This eleven-year-old kid with a snarl on his face where a smile should have been, my future husband's son, didn't care for me particularly. Ed had called Michael after dinner on Valentine's Day, right after he asked me to marry him, and Michael had responded to our news with uncharacteristic calm: "Congratulations. That's fine."

Then he added, "Just don't expect me to come to the wedding."

Ed replied that he really wanted Michael with us on such an important day and would be very sad without him, but the boy had to make his own choices. Soon, the polite tones gave way to pleading and tirades and yelling and name-calling and after about two hours, father and son hung up, hoarse and exhausted. Then Ed cried, I cried, and, as I found out later, Michael cried.

Not a particularly auspicious beginning to this new chapter of my life, especially when I had some doubts of my own. I was forty-four years old, divorced after twenty-six years of marriage and with a burgeoning international ministry to run. I was uncertain about taking on a new role as a stepmother, having almost finished raising four children of my own. My youngest was sixteen. Ed had a second son, Matthew, who was, thankfully, easy to please, but he was only six years old. God, I asked, do you really intend to send me backward ten years? My identity, or so I believed, was as a minister and the mother of grown children, not as a car-pool captain worried about the high cost of orthodontics. Besides, I'd been so sweet to this difficult child, even holding my tongue when he swore at the dinner table, something I'd never have tolerated from my own children. I smiled all the time. I smiled so much my face hurt.

My face hurt because a phony smile contorts our identity, and being untrue to ourselves causes pain. Often we lose our identity trying to please or placate others. We lose sight of who we are while trying to mesh our lives with those around us. We compromise our values and beliefs to make others happy or simply to avoid conflict. But when we dance around others or put on masks and costumes, we cannot achieve the clear and honest relationships that open the way to love.

Once, Ed dropped Michael off with me for the weekend so that his son could get to know my youngest son and me better. Michael stood in the front doorway, shoulders hunched, eyes downcast, as if weighted down by his backpack. He had his hands stuffed in the pockets of his jeans, and I had my left hand clasped in my right, as if in silent prayer. (The truth is I was covering my diamond for fear that it would catch the late-afternoon light and shine in Michael's eyes like a beacon of bad news.)

~~~~~~

I smiled all the time. I smiled so much my face hurt.

~~~~~~

I'd have done just about anything to avoid making that kid angry at me.

He finally pulled his hands out of his pockets to wave good-bye to his dad. Then Michael turned toward his future stepmother.

"Let's see it," he said, looking me in the eye for once.

I slowly unclasped my hands, holding out my left, as if for inspection. The single carat that had only hours earlier seemed subtly charming in its simplicity now looked showy and gaudy. Michael grasped my wrist with his left hand and began tugging at the ring with his right. Instinctively, I curled my finger.

"What are you doing?" I asked.

"Trying to pull it off," he responded, still tugging.

"And what would you do if you could?" I asked, momentarily grateful that Ed had bought a ring one size too small.

"Toss it down the disposal," he answered. Then he dropped my hand and without another word crossed over to the family room, where he plunked himself and his backpack down on the sofa in front of the Big Screen and reached for the remote. I started in on my speech about how I knew he already had a wonderful mother and how I didn't want to take her place, but I quit mid-sentence when he hit the volume button and *Star Wars* drowned me out.

The disposal. So that was where he thought his new family-to-be belonged. I'd been kind—excruciatingly nice, actually. Devastated by his parents' divorce, Michael was still a bit lost. He didn't fit in at school and rarely brought friends home. Under the circumstances, I could overlook his manners and behavior, I told myself; the poor guy had been through enough. Besides, I wanted him to like me. So without a word, I headed into the kitchen to start the potatoes for dinner—Michael's favorite, mashed russets—and took care not to peel directly over the disposal.

I managed to keep a smile plastered on my face not only that evening, but over the next few months, whenever Michael spent time with us. He would refuse to shower, brush his teeth or comb his hair, and I let it go. Inside, I'd be seething. I wanted him to shape up. But maybe if I let him get away with a few unhygienic habits, I thought, he'd warm up to me.

It didn't work.

How easily we are lured into a false identity. You know those times you tell people, "I'm just not myself today"? With Michael, I felt "not myself" all the time. I didn't know how to be a stepparent—or even if I *should* be one—so instead, I turned myself into what I thought Michael needed: Mother Nice. In return, Michael, uncertain of his own role and untrusting of this sweet-tempered fiancée of his father's, worked hard to make himself into someone he believed to be unlovable. When I asked him to clear his plate at dinner, he snarled, "You're not my mother," and went and plopped himself down in front of the TV with a bowl of Cheetos. He refused to do his homework. When Ed or I tried to encourage him to do his assignments, he'd respond that his teachers all thought he was stupid, so what was the point?

It was ten o'clock on a Saturday night a few months before Ed and I were to be married. I was just getting ready for bed when the phone rang. Sunday mornings, I'm up at four o'clock in order to put the finishing touches on my sermon and prepare for the busiest day of the week at church. Michael, now twelve, had been scheduled to spend the weekend with his father, but Ed had gone out of town on business unexpectedly, and I was called in to baby-sit. Naturally, Michael had sought escape as soon as possible and had been spending the evening at a video arcade with friends. He was expected home shortly, so I was surprised to hear his voice on the phone.

"Mary," he said, "I need you to come get me."

Had something happened? A friend's older brother was supervising. He had promised to drive the kids home by ten o'clock.

"I missed my ride," he explained.

"How did that happen?"

In a matter-of-fact voice, with no apology, he explained that his friend's brother had been ready to leave, but he had wanted to stay and finish his video game. "I told them to go because you'd come and get me," he finished.

The arcade was forty-five minutes away. My bathrobe was soft and warm. The comforter beckoned. After dressing and driving to and from the arcade, I wouldn't be back in my flannels until midnight at the earliest, giving me only a few much-needed hours of sleep. Michael knew this. He knew very well I got up at 4 A.M. on Sundays, but the Mary he knew, patience-of-a-saint Mary, who never got mad, who always ignored his insults and sullen attitude, would rush to his side without complaint. Not this time.

"How could you?" I demanded. "You know what time I have to get up in the morning. You were only thinking about yourself, weren't you? You . . ." and so forth. I was tired and grouchy and let it show.

I stopped, out of breath, and for a time the only noise on the end of the line was the distant hum of the Mario Brothers electronic jingle and an occasional explosion from Power Pete. Finally, Michael spoke up.

"Who *are* you and what have you done with Mary?" he asked. The Mary he knew would never have lost her temper. He considered the Mary he knew too good to be true—and in fact, he was right. This twelve-year-old, in his own way, had seen through my disguise. I wasn't the wicked stepmother of his imagination, but I wasn't Carol Brady, either. Being grouchy had actually felt quite good.

~~~~~~~~

"Who *are* you and what have you done with Mary?"

~~~~~~~~

Clearly, God had just offered me a gift: forty-five minutes on the freeway to figure out the person I intended to be with

Michael. What I truly wanted was a great relationship with my future stepson, but I wasn't going to forge that kind of bond by being someone other than my authentic self. In real life, I'm a person who discourages foul language and lackadaisical hygiene in my children. Yet until this moment, I had pretended to accept what had set me seething.

You cannot fake a relationship and feel right with yourself or anyone else. Changing yourself to fit what you think other people want doesn't work. Pretending to be someone other than yourself only broadens the distance between the person you are and the one with whom you're trying to establish closeness.

~~~~~~

Pretending to be someone other than yourself only broadens the distance between the person you are and the one with whom you're trying to establish closeness.

~~~~~~

Ask yourself, "Who am I?" Deep down, I know that I am a child of God who has inherited divine capacities; some of them I strive to develop, others are left languishing. I also have a human side. I lose my temper, lose patience and sometimes judge others and myself. My human side wants everybody to like me and on occasion has contorted my personality to feel more accepted. Those contortions get mighty uncomfortable, until I remember my true divine identity and return to myself.

We are all created in the image of our Creator—Love itself. There's no need to fake a relationship with God, because nothing I do can make my essential self more or less lovable. Why fake my way to closeness with a twelve-year-old boy? We have to be fully ourselves in order to have a fulfilling relationship with anyone else. Getting grouchy or losing patience or calling someone on inappropriate behavior are all part of our human experience. I deeply wanted to love Michael and wanted him to love me, but he sometimes behaved in ways I didn't like. If I couldn't even share that truth with him, what chance did we have?

As Michael crawled into the car at the video arcade that night, I silently asked, "God, what would Love do here? Help me to speak in a way that builds a bridge between my future son and me."

Months earlier, I had asked if it was God's will for me to raise more children when I'd already reared four of my own. "Why are You sending me back ten years?" I had asked. I hadn't waited for a response.

Driving along in the darkness that night with Michael at my side, I asked for guidance once again, only this time, I listened. I really listened. People often look at me quizzically when I talk about communicating with God. "Maybe it's because you're a minister, or can anybody do that?" they ask. The answer is, anybody can. We all receive messages from our Creator, but often we ignore Divine Guidance, simply because we're not really expecting God to show up in our lives or we haven't yet learned how to sense God's presence.

Think about the times you've waited at the airport gate for a loved one to arrive. One by one, passengers flow into sight. Your entire being is fixed upon those faces. Your attention is riveted. Announcements over the loudspeaker, the hum of the crowd all cease to exist. You are expecting that loved one to show up, and when he or she steps into view, a rush of recognition flows through your body and mind like adrenaline and you feel instantly lifted.

When we expect God to show up, our Creator never disappoints. God's presence, God's guidance, is readily distinguished from the babble in our brains as surely as our loved one stands out from the airport crowds. Recognition is instantaneous.

~~~~~~~~~

*God's presence, God's guidance, is readily
distinguished from the babble in our brains as surely
as our loved one stands out from the airport crowds.*

~~~~~~~~~

So this time, I stopped and listened, focusing on nothing but the message I knew would be forthcoming. Sometimes, those messages come in the form of signs, signals, even music, but at this moment, words reverberated in my mind as clearly as if someone standing next to me had actually spoken them: "Mary, I am not sending you back ten years. I am sending you forward."

My future with Michael began in that moment. Somehow I had thought that raising children was a job that I had already completed, that my purpose lay elsewhere. Now I understood that "going forward" meant a brand-new experience. Most of us don't like to admit to it, but loving somebody else's children can be more challenging than loving our own. That challenge, however, doesn't mean we love less—or less authentically. I was being invited to open my heart in a way I had never even fathomed.

"Michael," I said, "I know you didn't choose me to be your stepmom. I also know that you have a wonderful mom who loves you dearly and that you love her, too. I've been trying so hard to make you like me that I haven't been very real. Some of the things you've done and said have left me feeling hurt and angry, and I have always pretended that everything was fine, even when it wasn't. I know this may sound strange, but I'm sorry for not telling you when I was upset. From now on, I will, and I want you to be free to be real with me, too. I would really like it if we could start fresh, beginning right now."

Arms folded across his chest, Michael glanced sideways at me and nodded so slightly that a single blink would have made me miss the subtle inclination of his head. He didn't say anything the entire ride home, but the silence didn't feel hostile. It felt like a time for us both to think things over. And we did.

I would like to say that Michael and I never struggled again, but that would be the Brady Bunch. Our relationship did change, however. Michael not only attended our wedding, he asked to be the ring bearer. (No, he did not chuck the ring down the disposal.) Just before his dad and I exchanged vows, I glanced at him, standing proud in his rented tuxedo. I smiled at him and he winked and flashed a giant grin in my direction.

Michael went from being a boy who was feeling orphaned at home and outcast at school to being a kid who knew that wherever he found himself, he belonged. In the next few years, he would go on to be named Prince of his winter formal, voted most inspirational player on his football team and elected his new high school's first student body treasurer.

The first Christmas we spent as a new family, Michael, arms behind his back, came up to me and said, "I have a Christmas gift for you."

"Really? Do I get to open it now?"

He said, "No, it's not a gift I can wrap with paper. It's a gift I'm wrapping with my heart."

"What is this gift?"

He said, "I want to start calling you Mom."

You cannot pretend your way into a great relationship. I could not pretend to be an unflappable, all-forgiving saint and earn my stepson's genuine affection. I only became "Mom" by being me, a person who loves deeply and lets her human foibles show. God's love for us is not based on perfect behavior. God loves us because we belong to God. We are God's children. Yet we still nurture a belief that who we are isn't good enough.

Getting over feeling scared or ashamed of our true selves isn't easy. Yet every one of us has the capacity to grow into our potential as a loving being. Certainly, we all have the desire. Nobody sets out to make hiding a lifetime goal, although isolation is the place many people wind up. Why? Somewhere along the line, we assume an identity not our own, and the more time that passes, the harder it becomes for us to shed the disguise. Fear, condemnation, judgment, hesitation, manipulation become the masks that we wear, but the veneer of protection doesn't protect us at all: It only accomplishes what we least want—to create distance between ourselves, others and God. Just as a person using an alias must constantly look over his shoulder for fear of being identified, we never experience freedom until we own up to who we are.

Just as a person using an alias must constantly look over his shoulder for fear of being identified, we never experience freedom until we own up to who we are.

The more we open to our real selves, the more accepted we feel. I know these words are true, but I still have to remind myself at times. We can lose ourselves when we think our reward lies in somebody else's response. It's wonderful when somebody approves of us or responds the way we want, but real power comes from being ourselves.

If you've lost track of your own identity or fear rejection should that identity be revealed, know this: You are a unique expression of your Creator. There is not another being like you. You are an original. Nobody's got your thumbprint. Nobody's got your voiceprint. Nobody's got your soul print. You are an unrepeatable piece of the puzzle that is essential to the Divine plan. You have a very specific purpose, and that is to give your gift of love to the world. You are created in the image of God, and the essence of God is love. Whenever you align with your true self and reach out in a loving way, you are fulfilling your individual destiny.

~~~~~~~~~

There is not another being like you. You are an
unrepeatable piece of the puzzle that is
essential to the Divine plan.

~~~~~~~~~

"Who am I?" you ask. You are a child of God, born for a
glorious adventure in love.

~~~~~~~~~~~~~~~~~~

THOUGHTS THAT TRANSFORM

Finding perfect love in any relationship requires a transformation of
our thinking. Begin holding these thoughts each day:

~ My true identity is as a child of God. Why should I try to be anyone
  else?

~ Being my real self begins with my thinking. There's no greater
  investment I can make with my thinking than remembering my
  heritage.

~ With God, I am enough.

PRACTICE

*Pick a relationship that you would like to improve. It might be
with a parent, child, spouse, coworker or friend. The next time
you see or speak with that person, pause, take a deep breath
and ask the question, "What would Love do here?" And then
listen. Some idea will come to you, or perhaps a more
compassionate feeling will arise. Then act on that feeling.*

*Your rational mind may argue that this individual doesn't
deserve your love. Your ego may protest. (With my future*

stepson, I was initially more concerned about molding myself into someone he would like than I was about responding in an authentically loving way.) But this exercise is not about the other person. It's about discovering your own identity. At your core, you are not spiteful, manipulative or inadequate. You are a child of God, the essence of Love. The more you practice being authentically loving, the more your true identity is revealed.

2. NEVER ALONE

I know another Michael who struggled with discovering his true identity. When Michael was a young boy, his father died, and as a teenager he responded with anger that he had been abandoned. He started getting into trouble, growing sullen and disrespectful to teachers and his mother. Then one day, in the late 1960s, he attended an antiwar demonstration and saw a friend of his scuffling with a police officer. He started to head over that way and a policeman said to him, "You! Get outta here!"

Michael said, "Why? I haven't done anything."

Despite another warning, Michael kept pressing forward, and finally the policeman began to press in on him. Another officer joined him. Seeing that Michael was in trouble, friends gathered round, screaming, pressing, pushing, and the crowd seemed ready to explode.

Michael heard a voice inside of him saying, "Whatever you do, don't fight back." Yet as the noise around him escalated, Michael decided to ignore that voice. This was no longer about protesting the war in Vietnam or helping a friend. He could only think how good it always felt the instant his fist connected with a face that annoyed him. At that moment, Michael recalls, "I wanted to hit someone so bad and make everyone go wild."

A fire truck arrived, siren blaring. He and his friends might soon get hosed down. So Michael, heady with excitement and power, took a swing at the first uniform within his reach.

The next morning, sitting in a jail cell, Michael was greeted by a front-page newspaper headline that read, "Belligerent 16-year-old Incites Riot" and a message from the guard: Michael's mother wanted to see him. Two thoughts ripped through his mind at the same time: "Uh-oh" and "Bail?"

Imagine what a mother could say at that moment. "You shamed our family. What's wrong with you? You're just thinking about yourself. You shouldn't have been there. You've been in trouble before; now look what's happened."

But what this mother said to her son was something else entirely: "Michael, I don't know who you're pretending to be."

She went on, "Whoever you're pretending to be is not you. I know who you are." Then she began to recount the goodness that she had seen in him since early childhood. "You are that altar boy who loves God. You are that boy who cares about the other kids and helps out the ones who don't have any friends. You are that kid who . . . You are that kid who . . . You are that kid who . . ." She ended by saying, "And I want you to know . . .

"I want you to know there is nothing you can ever do that will cause me to stop loving you."

Then she left. Without paying bail.

Michael had three days to sit and consider his mother's words.

Those words never left Michael. On the cusp of manhood, he glimpsed, for the first time, that something about him might be more powerful than a balled fist. Years passed before he developed a relationship with God that was stronger than his own self-doubt or the anger over losing his father so young. Yet for Michael Moran, who would become a highly respected minister, the pivotal moment had occurred when he began to recognize that he could rise above his hurt and his mistakes.

"I'd always thought my mother's love wasn't big enough, because my dad wasn't there. It was just her," he recalls. "But when I realized how much she loved me, no matter what I did, that love seemed so much bigger. I wasn't alone. I figured out that if my mother loved me this much, maybe God loved me, too. Maybe I could do something better with my life, because I wasn't in this alone."

At any moment when we remember we are not alone, we tap into our innate capacity to triumph over a circumstance that would once have kept us down. In this way, we begin to discover our true identity as children of God.

> At any moment when we remember we are not alone, we tap into our innate capacity to triumph over a circumstance that would once have kept us down. In this way, we begin to discover our true identity as children of God.

In the ancient tombs of Egypt, archeologists found, among some of the mummies, seeds intended to grow food for the deceased in the afterlife. These seeds were then planted thousands of years later, and amazingly enough, they sprouted and bore fruit. A little nourishment was all they needed.

God seeded greatness in every one of us. Nourished by our attention and cooperation, the seed grows. But some of us don't nurture greatness. We nurture littleness instead. We let the seed lie dormant—that God Seed of the greatness that's within us— telling ourselves that unfortunate circumstances rule our lives. We write ourselves off: "I blew my chances," or "After an experience like that, I'll never trust again" or "I guess I just don't have what it takes."

Yet that *urge toward greatness* never goes away; it just gets covered under layers of disappointment and resignation. You can dig deep and begin to nurture the greatness within you at any time. God, from whose life you draw your own, is at the center of your being.

~~~~~~~~~

> God seeded greatness in every one of us. Nourished
> by our attention and cooperation, the seed grows.

~~~~~~~~~

With this awareness, begin to open to the truth: "Who I am is greater than this hurt. Who I am is greater than the problem before me, because I am never alone. God, my Higher Power, is only a thought away."

In First John 3:1, we read: "Behold what manner of love the Father has bestowed on us, that we should be called children of God!" What an incredible statement to absorb, that we are really the offspring of God! This means that the essence of who we are is divine and holy and coded for greatness. We are of divine lineage, and a part of us already recognizes the truth of this statement. But there's a chasm between who we really are and who we believe ourselves to be. The person we've accepted as ourselves is based on our past and what we've been told about ourselves by others. We've adopted the belief that we're not good enough, that something is missing. When everybody went through the line to get good looks and talent, we tell ourselves, we got stuck at the rear.

~~~~~~~~~

> In First John 3:1, we read: "Behold what manner of
> love the Father has bestowed on us, that we should be
> called children of God!" What an incredible statement
> to absorb, that we are really the offspring of God! This
> means that the essence of who we are is divine and
> holy and coded for greatness.

~~~~~~~~~

A number of years ago, I saw a show on television about a bear that gave birth to two cubs. One cub died almost immediately, and three weeks later, the mother bear died. One little cub was left to fend for himself. The narrator stated that a cub under such conditions, easy prey for predators on the lookout for a quick meal, typically lasts no more than ten days. Motherless cubs are like McDonald's, fast food of the forest. The camera offered a glimpse of a particularly hungry-looking mountain lion in the distance.

As the camera recorded the cub's every forlorn move, my heart lurched. (The dramatic music didn't help.) I tried reassuring myself: *They wouldn't have made a show about a cub that's going to die . . . would they?*

One day, the cub encountered a giant black bear. The little fellow seemed to cower at this giant's sheer mass, but the larger bear simply peered around, realized that Mom wasn't anywhere about and gave the cub a friendly nudge. The camera then followed the smaller bear happily trailing after the larger one; the adoption papers were clearly in order. Papa bear showed the cub how to grub for insects and fish and scratch his back against the bark of a tree.

One day, the two became separated. The cub looked about frantically for his new father, but couldn't find him.

Then, as the cub was approaching the stream where he'd learned to fish, something caught his attention. He looked up, and there stood that same mountain lion ready to pounce, the same cat that had been stalking his prey the entire show. No way would he have squared off with Papa bear, but now . . .

The camera zoomed in on the small cub, who automatically mimicked the posture of his adoptive daddy when threatened: He stood on his hind legs and bared his teeth. Then, in the tradition of his father, he set himself to let loose a mighty growl that would reverberate throughout the wilderness.

Of course, only a tiny squeak came out.

The camera shifted to the mountain lion; the end was near. How could I watch? But to my astonishment, the lion suddenly lowered his head and skulked off in the opposite direction.

The camera panned back to the proud little cub. Then we, as viewers, saw what the little fellow could not: that a few yards behind him, at full ferocious height on his hind legs, sharp white teeth bared in a protective snarl, stood Daddy bear. Even though the cub couldn't see his father, his father stood guard, protecting his young. That little cub had power available greater than anything he could manifest on his own.

That same Power is available to us. No matter how frightened or alone we feel, that doesn't mean the Spirit isn't here. That doesn't mean you aren't loved. We may feel separated from God, but God doesn't go anywhere. God is always with you, even when all you see are the bared fangs ahead. There is a Higher Power that right now wants only one thing for your life, that you grow and develop your capacity to live in the love in which you have been created.

The "Father" protects and provides for us. People who are connected consciously to God know that they have more than enough. We have more than enough ideas, more than sufficient inspiration, an abundance of internal resources to meet any situation. We have had access to God's love and support all along, because of our identity. We don't have to earn or perform to connect with God. That connection is ours because we are God's offspring. We don't have to adopt a different identity in order to be perfect or deserving. This wondrous identity as an individual child of God is not earned; it is a gift that lies in our hands.

I know something about you: You are a being who is made of pure love, because God created you. You are that one who has a divine purpose. You are that one who can make such a difference; for this you have been created. God is calling us each by name, saying, "There is a great purpose and a divine plan for your life. Everything you need is available to you. Partner with

Me by remembering and honoring your true self. You're not in this alone."

~~~~~~

Thoughts That Transform

~ I am not meant to live my life outside God's love.

~ As I become aware of my divine heritage, I increasingly feel the Presence of God in my life.

~ Where I am, God is, and I am never alone.

Practice

Begin using affirmations in your daily life. Affirmations are spiritual vitamins that, when ingested daily, help your thinking to grow more healthy. For instance, while it is true that we are God's children, we don't always feel that connection. That feeling of connection is derived from the thoughts we think.

Here are some affirmations that remind me of my heritage:

~It is never too late to be who I might have been.

~Behold what manner of love the Father has bestowed on me, that I should be called a child of God!

~Unseen and sometimes unfelt, God is nevertheless always with me.

Maybe these words don't quite ring true for you as yet. It doesn't matter. Choose one of these affirmations or another that attracts you in some way and tape it to your refrigerator or bathroom mirror—anyplace that you are likely to see it several times a day. You can choose affirmations from an endless number of sources. Whenever I read or hear something that sets off an inner spark, I jot it down. I've selected lines from movies, songs, literature and scripture. Sometimes, I enjoy making up my own affirmations. Why not keep your own affirmation notebook?

Make a habit of saying the words aloud whenever you see them. At first, you may feel like a child reciting the multiplication tables; you may think "they're just words." But over time, they'll become spiritual truths you'll find illustrated in day-to-day life.

You've had this experience before, although you may be unaware of it. Think of a song you loved as a teenager. The first time you heard it on the radio, the song barely registered. You may have thought "nice tune" or "catchy lyrics," but there was no excitement. Over time, however, you grew attached to the music. The words took on a special meaning. You turned up the volume whenever that song came on. You bought the album (or tape or CD). Today, whenever you hear that song, memories come flooding back to you. A spiritual affirmation enters your life in the same way, but it grows even bigger. While old music provides nostalgia, affirmations offer a kind of companionship. Words that once merely sounded nice resonate in your heart. Life begins to make more sense. You become increasingly aware: "I am not in this alone."

3. MADE TO RELATE

Remember the old Supremes song "You Can't Hurry Love"? Kathy was an expert at the opposite: postponing love. "When I get my career together, then I'll find a partner," she'd say. No matter who tried to date her, she was too busy. In college, scholastics came first. Later, work took precedence. And when she'd received yet another promotion and an old friend asked, "You seeing anyone now?" Kathy found refuge in flabby thighs. "I've been spending so much time at the office, I've really gotten out of shape. Once I start going to the gym for a while, then I'll be ready to let some man see me." Kathy had many acquaintances but few real friends. On the rare occasion a friend ventured to ask why Kathy never let men get close to her, she was genuinely surprised. "I'd love to meet someone," she'd say. "I'm just not ready yet." Or "I've just been so busy." She never sounded defensive or lonely, just matter-of-fact.

One day, however, she called the person she considered her closest friend, and her voice was shaking. "I've just been diagnosed with breast cancer," Kathy said.

The mastectomy was so radical, reconstruction was not an option. During the ensuing months of chemotherapy and radiation, Kathy began reflecting on her life. She realized that she had fooled herself into believing that her life had been too full to let love in, because in the absence of busyness, she felt unbearably empty. She returned to work as soon as possible, but climbing the corporate ladder no longer seemed as important. She wondered: *Who will ever love me now? I'm disfigured. I'm unlovable. And it may already be too late.*

After three years, however, the cancer had not returned. A new man joined Kathy's office and began to pay attention to her. She agreed first to lunch and later to dinner, but the new man's interest frightened her.

Her old friend told her: "You have never let anyone love you."

"I know," she said. "But the surgery . . ."

Her friend reminded her that prior to the surgery it had been fitness, and before that work, and before that . . .

So Kathy tried. She really tried. And the relationship progressed. Several months later, Kathy's coworker asked her to marry him, to which she responded, "I'm just not sure."

The two went off for their first weekend away together, to the mountains. When night fell, and the two sat cuddled before a fire, the moment came when he wanted to help her remove some of her clothing, and she pushed him away.

Finally, he looked her in the eye and said, "Why don't you quit hiding what you're trying to hide and just let me love you?"

In that moment, Kathy realized she had always been trying to hide. A part of her had been missing, not because of a mastectomy, but because of Kathy's belief that she was unlovable. She didn't believe a man would want to spend his life with her. Kathy wasn't even sure *she* wanted to spend her life with herself. She believed in God, but she didn't believe that God had any particular affection for her. When she heard the words "Why don't you just let me love you?" Kathy suddenly realized that all this time God had been ready to love her and she'd been the one holding back.

God says the same thing to each one of us: "Why don't you quit hiding and let me love you?" We try to hide whatever we think is unacceptable—a mistake we made in our past, limited education, our looks or the unkind thoughts we may harbor about others. Sometimes, we get so accustomed to being in hiding—or running and dodging and camouflaging—that we forget what it means to live life in the open.

We all have favorite haunts, places to which we retreat from relationship with ourselves, God and others. One popular hideout is a place called busyness. When we spend time here, we don't have time to relate to anything but the next item on our agenda. Some people escape into the world of acquisition. We willingly lose ourselves amid our belongings, confident that more means better. Others enter one relationship, then hide out from real commitment by escaping into another: "It just happened," they say with a shrug, as if they had no idea how they got there.

What makes these hiding places so alluring is that they each carry a payoff. Being busy brings us the pride of accomplishment; buying something new supplies a quick high; a new relationship brings temporary euphoria.

But we're never genuinely happy in hiding, because that is not how God intends us to live. Meaningful relationships thrive in an open environment in which love is given and received freely. If we want to experience perfect love, we've got to open up. Jesus told us that the greatest commandments were simply love: love of God, love of neighbor, love of self. The ultimate measure of who we know ourselves to be is what we express to others. If we're playing hide-and-seek, we cannot possibly be present for the very purpose we've been born, to learn and live in love.

~~~~~~~~

If we want to experience perfect love,
we've got to open up.

~~~~~~~~

God already knows everything about us and loves us uncon-
ditionally. That may sound hard to believe. Hiding a perceived
flaw feels like the most natural thing in the world; we've all been
teenagers mortified by bad skin. And nobody's blemishes look
quite so horrific as our own. But nothing we've ever done, nothing about us can be disguised from the One who created us.
We don't need a perfect complexion to receive the love of our
Creator.

Imagine someone handed you a clean, crisp twenty-dollar
bill. Now suppose someone handed you that same bill, only
crumpled and slightly torn. Would you value it any less? Of
course not. What happened to the bill doesn't change its worth.
God sees us the same way. No matter what happens in our lives,
we remain valuable to God.

It's as if God is saying, "Come close. Accept My love for
you. See yourself as I see you. In seeing yourself differently,
whatever you have found unlovable will melt away. Let Me love
you, so that you will know what it means to be loved; then let My
love extend to others through you."

We are not damaged; there's nothing essentially wrong or
missing that prevents us from living in love or loving relationships. As a child of our Creator, we are wired with an innate capacity for relationship, but we have to develop that capacity. No
matter your natural talent, fingers don't play Chopin the first
time they touch a piano. It takes practice. And over time, you
find that you have more to give than you could possible imagine.

We are not damaged; there's nothing essentially
wrong or missing that prevents us from living in love
or loving relationships. As a child of our Creator, we
are wired with an innate capacity for relationship, but
we have to develop that capacity.

Thoughts That Transform

~ There is nothing I can hide from God. My Creator already knows everything about me and loves me.

~ As I remember that I am loved absolutely, I lose the urge to hide.

~ God's love for me is not based on appearance or performance. God's love is unconditional.

Practice

Take out a piece of paper and list five reasons you believe yourself to be unworthy of absolute love. Remember, there's nothing to hide. This list remains between you and God, and God already knows. Does your body, your awkwardness in social situations, a low-paying job, or the fact that you rarely have a date for Saturday night embarrass you? When I first compiled such a list, this item ranked number one: I became pregnant at age sixteen and hurt the people I loved most.

Set the list aside for a moment. Settle back in a chair, take a couple of deep breaths, close your eyes and think of a precious young child, either your own, one you know or one you simply imagine. See this child's innocence and wonder at the world. Ask yourself if you believe a good parent would love this child less if he or she made a mistake or appeared physically less attractive than society's standards dictate. Look closely. I know this may be painful if your own parent was not so loving. But you know the truth—that a good parent's love for a child overlooks that child's blemishes.

Now, ask yourself: If I can imagine a human love that overlooks surface imperfection, how much more must my Divine Parent love me? At first, just consider the possibility that you may be so loved. Repeat this affirmation: "If a human parent can love greatly, how much more must my Divine Parent love me?"

As you spend time on a daily basis contemplating God's love, you open to the possibility of unconditional love with your name on it. Stay with the practice and you will begin to sense a gentle, judgment-free love that is not only with you, but for you.

CHOOSING TO LIVE IN LOVE

Spiritual Principle

You discover and develop the capacity for unconditional love in every one of your relationships. Within you is the power to live every day in love.

We never know how high we are,
Till we are called to rise;
And then, if we are true to plan,
Our statures touch the sky.

—EMILY DICKINSON

4. WHAT I SEE STARTS IN ME

My mother always outdoes herself on Thanksgiving, but one year, the meal surpassed all others, with melt-in-your-mouth honey-glazed turkey and pecan stuffing so intoxicatingly fragrant, I couldn't resist another little scoop from the bowl every time it passed in my direction, which was often. What with all the other goodies—cranberry sauce, sweet potatoes, rolls and salad coated with creamy Caesar dressing—a miniature Mount St. Helens towered on my plate. When dessert rolled around, I knew better than to accept a second slice of pumpkin chiffon pie, but the scent of warm, sweetened cinnamon wafting under my nose . . .

"Make it a small piece," I cautioned my mom, an instruction she promptly ignored. I polished off every last crumb.

I'm a petite woman, but at this particular juncture in my life, I weighed about ten pounds more than usual, and after putting away a week's worth of calories in a single sitting, I felt ready to explode. Why, I lamented, did I even bother putting that pumpkin pie in my mouth? I could have applied it directly to my hips. My skirt, a size larger than I normally wore, felt uncomfortably tight, and I was looking forward to going home, putting on my robe and vowing to start a diet the next day.

As we headed out the front door, my sister-in-law smiled, looked me straight in the eye and said the meanest thing anyone could have in that moment: "You look like a Butterball."

A Butterball. I looked like a big, fat, overstuffed turkey. I had already been uncomfortable with my appearance, but this was outrageous. Not saying a word, I marched right to my car and slammed the door, seething. But I went to bed that night afraid to look in the mirror. Unable to sleep, I lay awake, reeling over her snide comment. "Why would she say that to me!? I don't look that fat," I thought.

"Or do I?"

I finally told myself, "Mary, you need to forgive this."

Eventually. Maybe. But for the time being, I needed to stew in my own juices, so to speak. My sister-in-law wasn't exactly a size 4 herself, and I'd noticed that her second slice of pie was about as big as mine. What gave her the right to act so superior?

The next morning, carefully dressed in a loose-fitting black dress (black is a slimming color), I went to confront her. She'd barely opened the front door when I burst out: "I know I've gained some weight, but how could you say that to me? That really hurt my feelings."

She looked at me blankly. "When did I say what?"

I said, "You know very well when. Last night, when we were leaving, you told me I looked like a Butterball."

She scrunched up her brow a moment, as if perplexed, then burst out laughing. "Mary, what I said was, 'Would you LIKE a Butterball?' It was a joke. We'd all eaten so much, the last thing any of us wanted was more turkey. Get it? A joke!"

What I heard was not what she had actually said but the message I'd already been conveying to myself. All the negative thoughts and feelings I'd been harboring about my appearance had risen to the surface, only I'd voiced them through my sister-in-law. My mind told me I'd overindulged, so I saw—and heard—evidence to support my belief.

My sister-in-law was incredibly rude to me. It was a horrible experience, only it never happened, except in my own mind.

"You say you've gained some weight?" she continued. "Where? It sure doesn't show."

What I see starts in me. My sister-in-law seemed to be condemning me because I was already condemning myself. Whatever our experience, the lens through which we see it is colored by our beliefs. If I believe relationships are troubled, the experience I create will prove me right. I will, inevitably, find trouble in a current relationship. Your partner or spouse may make a totally innocent comment that you will twist and mold to conform to the most outrageous belief.

~~~~~~~

It was a horrible experience, only it never happened, except in my own mind.

~~~~~~~

A woman friend of mine who'd been painfully hurt over past rejections had met the man of her dreams. After taking her out for an elegant dinner one night with a group of other couples, he brought Lori home, then said he had to leave because he needed to be at work early the next morning. "In fact," he said, "I've got such a crazy, busy next few days at the office, I don't think I'm going to be able to see you this week."

It was Sunday, 10:30 P.M., really not all that early, but in Lori's mind, her new boyfriend had cut the evening short. She promptly dismissed the elaborate dinner and the rare French wine he'd ordered to celebrate the evening. Given the tremendous amount of time the two had been spending together lately, when he said, "I'm not going to be able to see you this week," Lori heard, "I'm dumping you. I'm nicer than your past boyfriends, so I'm rejecting you in a really, really classy way, but get the message, woman: We're through."

On the verge of tears, Lori all but shoved her now bewildered boyfriend out the door. Since he genuinely did have an unusually busy week ahead, it had never occurred to him that saying so would upset Lori. He knew about Lori's history of being rejected—she'd confided in him two days earlier—but since dumping her wasn't what he was doing, he didn't think to reassure: ". . . but I'll be thinking of you, and I'll call every night."

Lori saw what she believed to be true, that any man who got to know her would eventually leave. The poor fellow, who hadn't a clue what was going on, went home, and for the first time had second thoughts about the relationship. Just as Lori had known he would.

Now ask yourself, which party erred? Was Lori's boyfriend, who couldn't possibly have forgotten about her past in just forty-eight hours, an insensitive lout? Was Lori amiss for jumping to the wrong conclusion? The answer is, it doesn't matter. We don't respond to objective facts but to what we perceive to be the truth.

In the movie *Sleepless in Seattle,* Annie is a single journalist played by Meg Ryan who becomes incensed when a coworker repeats the popularly reported statistic that shot fear through America's single female population: that women over forty were more likely to be killed by a terrorist than to get married. Annie points out that the statistic had turned out to be untrue, to which her editor, Becky, played by Rosie O'Donnell, quickly responds, "It's not true, but it feels true."

If it "feels true" that your partner will reject you, then, like Lori, you will seek out a Dumpster with your name on it at every corner. Try to remember that the "facts" of your life carry no more weight than the meaning you attach to them. Facts change and can be examined from alternate angles and possess no more power over us than the credence we give them. If we believe they are powerful enough to stop us, they halt our progress. If we look higher, if we look for what I call the "God thought" behind every action and intention, nothing in the world can stop us from surging ahead.

〰〰〰〰〰〰

The "facts" of your life carry no more weight than the meaning you attach to them.

〰〰〰〰〰〰

What do I mean by a "God thought"? Consider the Hindu story about the traveler who comes across an aged wise man sitting on a curb just outside a small town. He stops and asks, "Wise man, tell me, what kind of people are in this city?" to which the elderly man responds: "Tell me of the people who dwell in the city from which you came."

The newcomer sits down, scrunches up his face and issues a litany of complaints: "Oh, they were horrible: mean, nasty, self-centered. They were always thinking about themselves."

The wise man says, "You know, the same people live in this city." Upon hearing this, the visitor quickly gathers his belongings and sets off in search of friendlier territory.

Not long after, another traveler approaches the edge of town and encounters the wise man: "Tell me," he asks, "what kind of people are in this city?" And the older fellow again poses this question: "What kind of people dwell in the city from which you came?"

"Wonderful people, kind people, generous people, the most considerate you could imagine."

"Those same people are in this city." So the traveler enters the village, confident of his welcome.

We create the "kind of people" we live with every time we ascribe motives to their behavior. Is the person who reaches out his hand giving or grabbing? The first traveler contains all our human doubts and fears. The second traveler represents our divine side. God sees the good in every single one of us and knows the positive intention behind each behavior. First Corinthians states that "love believes the best" about others and ourselves.

Believe the best. Whatever image your mind clings to will tend to replicate itself in your real world. Lori, for example, believes the worst. She recognizes how fear of rejection sends men packing, but she can't seem to stop herself. "One of these days I know I'm going to jump to a conclusion, miss, fall and break my neck," she says. "But what can I do?"

Like many people, Lori wants to attract love into her life but winds up repelling it instead. Outwardly confident, she secretly regards herself with contempt. No one has received more bouquets of flowers or been pursued with more ardor than Lori. Her looks, her humor and her giving nature have been praised to the hilt. But no romance has ever lasted, leaving her feeling as if she must be utterly unlovable. Just when she gets her hopes up that a man she cares about will stick around, he leaves—never neglecting to tell her just what a wonderful person she is. "It's fine to be admired," she says, "but all I've ever really wanted is to be loved." Pained by seeing happy couples on her block, at the supermarket or in the movie theatre, she wonders: "Why not me? If there was something about me that I could fix, I would. But I don't even know what's wrong with me that I can't have what everyone else seems to take for granted."

Is Lori unworthy of love? Of course not. But her negative feelings about herself, her anticipation that she will be rejected— and her anxious efforts to hold on to love—may be sending the wrong message. What she told her boyfriend couldn't help but make him feel guilty and pressured, emotions that are a precursor to rejection. Guilt and pressure may also have wiped out his memory of their wonderful evening together. He might have left thinking: "Wow. I must be this woman's whole life. I'm not ready for that kind of responsibility."

Imagine that Lori instead had simply taken her partner at his word. Suppose she'd told him, "Thanks for letting me know you'll be busy. It was a great evening and I'll miss you this week, but I hope all goes well for you." He would have left with nothing other than the memory of a lovely time together and would probably have tried to call her as soon as he had time.

Unless Lori learns to let herself feel God's love—the only love truly big enough to satisfy the soul—she will always pull too hard on others, wanting them to fill a hole she feels in her own soul. The very pressure we put on others to be close is actually what drives them away. By contrast, when we ourselves feel full, we naturally become more attractive to others. We don't relate out of a deficit, but because we have so much to share. With this knowledge, Lori might find words that resonate within her soul, letting her know that she is worthy. Then, as a person who is innately lovable, she will begin to gain confidence that her boyfriend isn't about to bolt. Even if the relationship doesn't last, Lori will not feel so abandoned. The companionship of her Creator will fill her in a way that a boyfriend never can, and the need to grasp or cling will fall away.

The very pressure we put on others to be close is actually what drives them away. By contrast, when we ourselves feel full, we naturally become more attractive to others.

There is a part of Lori's story that belongs to every one of us. The love we try so hard to squeeze from someone else can only be found within. Once it is discovered, we can share and celebrate that love with others. I'm reminded of an ancient saying: The light you seek is within your own lantern.

Seek out the God thought, and you begin to attract opportunities, ideas and people in harmony with that mental attitude. A

God thought doesn't deny the reality of a behavior or way of living that is destructive. A God thought removes the filter that dims reality and allows every positive intention to shine through. God has blessed you with the capacity for great relationships. We may stumble and fumble, blinded by what we think we see in others—the real turkey at that Thanksgiving dinner was me—but God also gave us the power to pause, ask for guidance and then look again.

~~~~~~~~~

A God thought removes the filter that dims reality and allows every positive intention to shine through.

~~~~~~~~~

Turkeys can transform, and "the kind of people" who live in our relationships really can be the best in all the world.

~~~~~~

Thoughts That Transform

~ I choose to "believe the best."

~ When I see myself as "unacceptable," I'll create an experience that validates my self-deprecation.

~ When I see myself as God sees me, I come to know that I am loved.

Practice

Whenever you find yourself hurt, disappointed or feeling judgmental in any relationship, remember that another perspective is always available. Pause; ask deeply, "What is a God thought regarding this?"

A God thought is any thought that believes the best about

yourself or someone else. No matter how readily you believe that thoughts pop into your head of their own accord, you really do choose what takes up space in your mind. Often, a second opinion is warranted. A God thought allows you to lift your own thought to meet that of God's. A God thought assumes a person's best intentions, as opposed to the worst. A God thought will help you avoid jumping to erroneous conclusions about yourself and how others see you.

5. By Design, Not Default

Flying home to Portland from a conference in Chicago, I was seated next to a man, who, with a little help from his friend Jack Daniel's, poured out his life story, the latest chapter of which was getting under way just over the Rockies. Earning just shy of a million dollars a year at age thirty-eight, Bob is the number five man in an $8 billion company, and Bob's father cannot fathom why his son is not number one. Bob and his wife have a full-time nanny for their two children and vacation in Europe or the Bahamas every year. The couple owns a condo on the coast that sits vacant most of the year unless they loan it to friends, but they don't rent it out because Bob's wife feels queasy about having strangers amongst their belongings. Bob is adamant about selling the place, because the taxes are ridiculous and when was the last time they went to the beach? His wife has fond memories of the condo and likes the idea of knowing it's there, just in case.

I mention the condo conundrum because it's apparently the most heated and passionate discussion Bob and his wife have had in a long time, which tells me something about the state of their relationship.

"I've been married thirteen years, and my wife and I never talk about anything but the business of the house and the kids and where we'll go on vacation. In a few years, when the kids are grown, I'm afraid my wife and I will look at each other and see strangers," he told me.

Bob let out a giant sigh and turned to me as if he'd run out of steam and felt compelled to revert to small talk. "So, what do you do?"

"I'm a minister," I said. Over the years, having seen many strangers respond to this revelation, I knew what Bob would do next.

He clammed up. I saw him mentally flip through the last hour, searching for anything he wouldn't have uttered to a woman of the cloth. And then he did what most people do when I meet them on airplanes, which was to ask for advice. "I want my relationship with my wife to be better. I want my relationship with my father to be better," he said. "But I don't know how."

I suggested to him that achieving number five status in such a successful company at such a young age must have taken a great deal of creativity and ingenuity.

He modestly agreed. "Early on, I had this great idea, and then I fine-tuned it along the way and . . ."

The conversation began to get a little technical for me, so I gently interrupted, "You've really directed your creativity at work. Did you know you have the same opportunity with your personal relationships?"

"What do you mean?"

I explained to Bob my belief that as children of God, we're born creative. In our professional lives, we might direct creativity toward material success, toward manifesting a dream or helping to further a cause. But sometimes, we forget that the same natural ability we fine-tune in that aspect of our lives can help us succeed in what matters most: building great relationships. I asked him to think about how much energy he devoted to his job, how often he stayed awake nights strategizing or drumming up a new idea, how excited he became when that idea was transformed into reality.

"By partnering with God," I told him, "you could design your relationships the same way you've designed your career."

Bob seemed intrigued. He jotted down a few notes. And then, just as our plane touched down in Portland, when the reality hit him that his marriage might actually change if he made the effort, Bob balked.

"You know, our marriage may not be all that great, but we're probably not any different from most people. We get by."

I hope that one day Bob changes his mind. Perhaps he'll realize that he doesn't have to settle for a mediocre marriage, because to do so would squander his God-given gift. What does "God-given gift" mean? The first mention of God in the Bible is as Creator. "In the beginning God created the heaven and the earth." Then a few verses later, we read, "And God said, let us make man in our image." If God is introduced as Creator and if the initial reference to humanity is that we are made in the image of God, then our essential nature is creative.

This truth is not limited to the Judeo-Christian Bible. Teachings in the *Tao te Ching* tell us: "I am a child of God. I came from the womb of creation." *A Course in Miracles* says: "Because of your likeness to your Creator, you are creative."

We are creative. What we do with our creativity—indeed, whether or not we even perceive our own creative ability—is another matter. Small children instinctively recognize their creativity. I remember proudly bringing home finger paintings from kindergarten, fully expecting Mom and Dad to treat my creations as masterpieces, and they did. My gallery was the refrigerator door, with exhibits changing weekly, sometimes daily, depending on my productivity. And heaven forbid my parents should have tried to discard any of my work, even if it amounted to no more than a few slashes of pencil on a piece of notebook paper. Throwing my artwork away would have been tossing out a piece of me. And they knew it.

But God didn't endow us with creative capacity just so Bob could succeed at business or children could finger-paint. We are meant to direct our creativity toward building better relationships. No longer do we have to struggle endlessly or settle or sit by. We have the power to make relationships great.

What is a "great" relationship? You can connect with another in such a way that you both feel more alive. The world seems more vivid. Food tastes better. Mundane chores don't seem so dreary. You can awaken each morning and move through each day with the unshakable assurance, "It doesn't get much better than this." A great relationship means that the very sound of a loved one's voice fills you with joy. Looking at the face of a spouse or partner, you marvel, "How did I get so lucky?" even after you've been together for forty years.

I know a man who sent a card to his wife while he was on a business trip, reading, "My beautiful Julie. I love you and miss you so much. I am the luckiest man to have found you. If there is such a thing as eternity, I want to go through it with you."

One might assume that Julie and her husband are newlyweds and that his trip was a lengthy one. In fact, they've been married thirteen years, and he was gone all of four days.

~~~~~~~~~~

No longer do we have to struggle endlessly or settle or sit by. We have the power to make relationships great.

~~~~~~~~~~

You thrill to the good times, but remain heartened during tough times, because of the support that sees you through them. You take tremendous pride in the other person's accomplishments, as if they were your own, and feel the pang of their hurt, too. I know one mother who, when her son was little and had the flu, would hold his head over the toilet, saying, "I'm so sorry; I wish it were me," because she would gladly have vomited for him to spare her little boy that discomfort. Now an adolescent, when down with the flu he still asks, "Do you wish it were you?" And his mother's answer is still a resounding "Yes."

When your most intimate relationships thrive, you are filled with a sense of well-being and fulfillment that cannot help but spill over onto others. You want to treat neighbors, coworkers and the busboy at the restaurant with kindness and respect. It's no accident that Julie, whose husband writes loving notes, is an active volunteer at her children's school, delivers meals to shut-ins and has a thriving circle of close friends. When one of those friends is feeling deeply troubled, Julie has been known to call several times a day and show up with a homemade dinner.

~~~~~~~~~

When your most intimate relationships thrive, you are filled with a sense of well-being and fulfillment that cannot help but spill over onto others.

~~~~~~~~~

Start by taking a good look at the people in your life. If you have a partner, are the two of you closer after five or ten years than on the day you wed? Do your children trust and confide in you? If you're without a partner, do you value being with yourself? How readily do you tell your own parents, "I love you"? Are your workplace relationships filled with respect, easy camaraderie, creative collaboration? Do you have the kind of friends who drop everything when you really need them? Are *you* that kind of friend?

It's not as if we have no desire for deeply fulfilling relationships or lack the natural creativity to bring them into being. Yet with so many people in the world, loneliness remains pervasive. How can that be?

Nobody designs a mediocre life. A mediocre life is lived by default, by drifting. Nobody getting married plans on being lonely. No one plans to cause an automobile accident. No one steps into a bar and plans to become an alcoholic. No one has children and plans on being so busy that the kids grow up strangers. Nobody plans to be hurt, becoming so embittered a grudge gets nursed to the grave. No one finds religion and plans on turning self-righteous. Nobody plans to live by default or drift, but it happens.

Fulfilling relationships happen by design, not default. Just because we're naturally creative doesn't automatically render us Picassos. We create whatever we focus on. We can create relationships that are fulfilling and life-giving. Or we can create confusion, excuses and copies of what we've always known.

> Fulfilling relationships happen by design, not default.

When we proceed through life not mindful of our purpose, we get into all kinds of trouble, as I discovered one dark Sunday morning while driving to church. I was rushing down a dark lane when seemingly out of nowhere a patrol car fell into line behind me. It was 5:30 A.M. This was the third time this had happened in as many months.

"Do you know why I stopped you?" the officer asked.

Two months earlier, I'd run a stop sign, and the officer had let me off with a warning. Last month, I'd received another warning for having my brights on.

I smiled, unaware of my present transgression. "I'm going to church. I was thinking about the scripture I'm using today. Did I tell you I'm a pastor?" The speech had worked like magic the last two times.

Unlike his predecessors, however, this man in blue was unimpressed. He did not care why I had broken the law, only that I had been going 40 mph in a 25-mph zone. He wished me luck on my sermon, handed me a ticket and drove off.

This being my first offense—on paper, at any rate—I had the opportunity to attend traffic school and have the infraction erased. There were forty of us in class. We paid for the course and gave up four hours of an afternoon, but our records were cleansed of any misdeed.

The teacher's name was Mr. Lord. (Really.)

Until then, the warnings I'd received had impacted me momentarily, but soon my old patterns would resurface, because deep down I believed that my sermon was more important than concentrating on the road. I didn't deliberately flash my brights, cruise through stop signs or exceed the speed limit, but all those things occurred. If I fail to stop, that means I'm not pausing to really be present to my surroundings. And if I speed . . .

The Lord—in the form of *Mr.* Lord—was saying to me, "Slow down, Mary. Pay attention."

We direct creativity like a car. Pay attention and that car will take us very quickly where we want to go; drive without focusing and we're an accident waiting to happen.

We direct creativity like a car. Pay attention and that car will take us very quickly where we want to go; drive without focusing and we're an accident waiting to happen.

Mr. Lord gave each of us a checklist so we'd become more aware of our habits and more likely to change the bad ones. Have you stopped recently to examine the patterns in the way you relate to others? Sometimes our patterns become so deeply ingrained, we drive through our relationships on automatic pilot until an "accident" jolts us awake.

Aristotle said: "We are what we repeatedly do. Excellence, then, is not an act, but a habit." That is, we need to think about what we can do on a daily basis to strengthen our relationships and then remind ourselves to actually do them. We can leave for work each morning waving "Good-bye!" to our spouse over our shoulder, or we can take a few seconds to look him or her in the eye and say, "I love you" or "I'll miss you today." It's a minor shift, but imagine how over time, a simple declaration of feeling could enrich your partnership. On a daily basis, we can certainly find a few minutes of one-on-one time for each child. Wouldn't they feel more loved and valued, and grow a healthier self-esteem?

I know a woman whose pattern was to bicker with her sons. She loved them dearly, but she also had very precise expectations for their behavior. Ever since her boys were little, whenever they failed to do as she expected, she would immediately point out their faults. They would sulk or snap back, and another argument would ensue. The pattern of struggle was so deeply ingrained, it felt almost inevitable.

———〰〰〰———

Some people live ninety years, and some live one year ninety consecutive times. With God's help, you really can alter the patterns that no longer fit the life you choose to design for yourself.

———〰〰〰———

One summer, her sons—now grown men—scheduled vacations to see her. When the younger son arrived, the mother's mouth dropped open. She hadn't seen him for a year and a half, and in that time, her clean-cut baby had turned into an unshaven freak. His hair, streaked blue, was long enough for a ponytail. His clothes looked like Goodwill rejects. He came in, sat down and started to talk to her. She was ready to pounce, thinking, "This isn't how I raised you. You look like a criminal. What happened to you?"

She stopped herself just in time. In the past year, lonely since her younger son had left, she had been working on getting closer to God. During this time, she had come to recognize her creative capacity and to see that she had the power to create a different kind of relationship with her children. Now she asked for God's help in forging that relationship. As she did so, the words filled her mind: "Does your son have to look the way you think he should in order for you to love him and listen to him?"

"But the blue hair . . ."

And she had to ask herself: "Which do I want more? To be right about my son's hair color or to have a better relationship with him?" So she sat down next to him and said nothing judgmental. She listened to his stories about work and friends and never once criticized his appearance. It was a glorious visit, and she learned more about her son that week than she had in the past decade.

Two weeks later her firstborn son arrived. She breathed a sigh of relief as he pulled up in a fancy car, wearing a three-piece suit and designer tie. Clean-shaven and smiling, he carried a leather briefcase.

"Wow! Doesn't he look good!" she thought. The son kissed his mother on the cheek, walked in, sat down and turned on the television. "How was your trip . . . ?" she began, but he only clicked the remote. Frustration mounted. Here she'd anticipated his visit for months, and all he cared about was channel surfing.

Mom was primed to bicker. "You can watch TV anytime. How often do you get to see your mother?" she wanted to say. Instead she paused, asked God for help and remembered that she had the creative capacity to break her pattern and design a new relationship. "Does my son have to behave in a certain way for me to love him and just be with him?" she asked herself. So she joined him on the sofa and commented only on the shows they watched.

When the weekend ended, her son gave her a hug, a tighter, longer hug than he had since he was a child. "Mom," he said, "my job has been so stressful; I've got people coming at me all the time, and I feel like I have to be this superhuman person and impress everyone. I can't tell you how good it felt this weekend to just be with you and relax and not worry what anyone thought of me. I could just let go with you, and it was great."

Some people live ninety years, and some live one year ninety consecutive times. With God's help, you really can alter the patterns that no longer fit the life you choose to design for yourself. You do not have to drift. You will not change all at once, but progress is more important than perfection. God, who passed on to you the gift of creativity, isn't done with you yet.

~~~~~~~~~~~~~~~~~~~~~~

THOUGHTS THAT TRANSFORM

~ Fulfilling relationships happen by design, not default.

~ I design my relationships as a cocreator with God.

~ In order to change unhealthy relationships, I need to first notice where I'm drifting.

~ I can develop new patterns that help me to create the relationships I truly want.

~ God didn't create me for mediocrity. God offers the experience of greatness through my relationships.

PRACTICE

Ask a loved one to be candid with you about a pattern in your relationship that may be causing some distance. When I asked my adult children this question, every single one of them answered identically: THE CELL PHONE! "Mom, your phone interrupts our visits and we end up feeling less important than your work," my daughter said.

When I do this exercise at retreats, a spouse will frequently mention the tendency to interrupt as a troublesome pattern. "He always cuts me off," or "I feel like she only cares about what she has to say because she never lets me finish a sentence."

The person who has been interrupted usually responds in one of three ways: struggling (fighting to gain control of the conversation), settling (accepting the fact that he or she won't be heard) or sitting by (tuning out of the relationship, no longer even aware of the interruption). Bit by bit, the relationship is eroded.

If you were the interrupting spouse at my retreat, I would ask your partner to promise not to mention the pattern for an entire week. This exercise is not about putting you in the wrong.

Then I would ask you to commit to being attentive to the behavior causing the distance:

~Each time you catch yourself, write it down in a notebook. Quite frankly, I was certain my kids had exaggerated my phone time, until I jotted down every call that came in when I was with them and how long each call pulled me away from their company. Ouch! I was appalled by how I had allowed work to intrude on my sacred time with family.

~Begin and end each page of your notebook with an affirmation, anything that lifts you up and reminds you of your true heritage. (It's a good idea to fill these in ahead of time, when the notebook is still blank.) You can choose something from scripture or an inspirational quote, anything that lifts and reminds you of your divine heritage. My favorite is quite simple: "With God, all things are possible." That reminds me I've got a powerful partner in change.

~Spend some time reviewing the depth and breadth of your patterns. One woman at a retreat not only discovered that she never let her mate finish a sentence, she cut off her coworkers *as well, including a supervisor. (And she'd been wondering why she was passed over for promotion.)*

~*Seek to alter your patterns. As a minister, I want to remain available for emergencies, but it had reached the point that everyone automatically dialed my cell if they couldn't reach me at home. Now, I've recorded an emergency pager number on my home phone to discourage routine calls to my cell. I have also learned to push the "off" button on my cell, which has given the "on" signal to my loved ones.*

6. A Picture of Greatness

More than anything, my friend Mark desired to find his life's partner. He dated a succession of seemingly kind, successful, intelligent women, but they never stuck around for long.

"I thought men were the ones who were supposed to be commitment-phobic," Mark used to say, "but the women I fall for can't seem to get out of the relationship fast enough. What is it with these women, anyway?"

A deeply spiritual man, Mark grew slightly resentful that his friends' relationships thrived while God allowed his to flounder.

Then he met Marie. She was the one; he just knew it, although he couldn't seem to help himself from constantly fretting, "What if she leaves me, too?" With their busy lives, they didn't have an opportunity to spend much time together, so Marie offered to plan a vacation for the two of them. Working around Mark's schedule—he lectures across the country—she picked a week in April and rented a cottage on the Oregon coast. Surely, Mark would be thrilled by the romantic getaway.

Unfortunately, he had Hawaii on his mind. "What were you thinking?" Mark snapped at her. "The beach? In April? This is the Pacific Northwest, honey. Anyone with half a brain knows there's nothing to do but stare at wet seagulls down there this time of year."

When Marie became upset at his outburst, Mark responded, "You're just being emotional."

"No," she said. "I'm being smart." Marie kept the reservation and went to the beach—by herself.

Mark had a week to fume and to rehearse his hurt. "She's just like all the others," he told himself. But as he began to relive past relationships, the women's parting words came back to haunt him. The same adjectives had been applied to him not once, but many times. "You're so self-centered, so arrogant," one partner had told him as she'd announced a reconciliation with her old boyfriend. "I am not self-centered," Mark had countered, immediately thinking of some magnanimous act to dismiss her claim. "Do you feel anything at all?" asked another as she closed the door for the last time.

"I most certainly do," Mark thought now. "I feel lonely." "You know," he told himself, "the one common denominator in all these broken relationships isn't the women. It's me."

Mark had been brought up by a domineering father who treated Mark's mother little better than a servant. Mark got the message early on that men are innately superior to women. He now knew this belief was wrong, but his behavior remained rooted in old patterns. Mark would override his partners' decisions, interrupt and say, "Now, if you'd only thought this through . . ." then eventually wind up feeling abandoned as these women whom he had treated condescendingly inevitably left him.

The thought that he might have lost Marie panicked Mark. He packed a bag and was halfway out the door, ready to zip down to the coast and apologize profusely, when he stopped himself. The reunion would be bliss, but sooner or later, the relationship would fail, just like all the others. And this time, his heart would truly be broken.

Mark realized he needed a power stronger than his own to

bring about the kind of loving, lasting relationship he desired. He couldn't turn to a friend, because Mark considered himself stronger than everybody he knew. There was a Presence, however, whose power he recognized as infinite, and that was God. He had turned to God for strength in other aspects of his life—his relationship with his parents, problems at work—but it had never before occurred to him that God could assist with his love life.

Through prayer and meditation, Mark thought more deeply about his relationship with Marie. He began to realize that his frame of reference was failure. In the back of his mind, he expected Marie to follow the lead of her predecessors, which ate away at his confidence. The more his confidence faltered, the harder he tried to boost himself the way he always had, by demeaning his partner.

Mark knew that everything is first created in one's mind before it can take form, but he hadn't applied that kind of thinking to his relationships before. Now he saw that he'd been pouring his creative energy into a vision of hopelessness, and that his relationship with Marie replicated the picture in his mind. Maybe he had even created loneliness by focusing on precisely what he least wanted to happen.

> Everything is first created in one's mind
> before it can take form.

Mark decided that there had to be a better way. He asked God to help him recognize when he had thoughts of superiority over Marie. As he continued to ask for help, a picture appeared in his mind of the two of them standing on balance scales. He noticed when certain thoughts tipped the scales in his favor— whenever he interrupted or corrected her—and tried to imagine how those scales would look in equilibrium. In his mind—before he spoke—he kept shifting weight back to her so that she could feel as valued and respected as she deserved to be. He created a mental picture of the kind of relationship he so deeply desired, with him and Marie as equal, loving partners. He imagined what it would feel like to be wrong about something, and he imagined Marie forgiving him.

Mark practiced his mental imaging while Marie was at the coast, so that by the time she returned, he felt confident enough to share with her that he was making a sincere effort to improve their relationship. Skeptical at first, Marie came to be touched by the newfound energy he was pouring into the relationship. By asking for the highest vision possible of this relationship, Mark created a mental picture of Marie as his wife. A year later, I watched as that image took form at the altar of his church.

Mark had transformed his life through the spiritual practice of creating what's known as a "mental equivalent," a process described by spiritual teacher Emmet Fox in the 1930s. Trained originally as an engineer, Fox always constructed a mental image of how anything he built would work. Recognizing that his thought process guided the scientific process, he believed the same to be true in other parts of his life as well. Fox believed that our lives reflect the pictures we create in our minds, and that therefore we should pay close attention to our mental doodling.

He wrote: ". . . for anything that you want in your life—a healthy body, a satisfactory vocation, friends, opportunities, and above all, the understanding of God—you must furnish a mental equivalent. Supply yourself with a mental equivalent and the thing must come to you. Do not supply the mental equivalent and you have no hope of bringing that desired good to you."

We are creating all the time through our thoughts. The

mind is inventing one thought or another twenty-four hours a day, even as we sleep, but few of us pause long enough to reflect upon our mental creations. Whatever image our mind clings to will tend to replicate itself in our real world. Unfortunately, many of us create what we least want by holding on to poor images.

~~~~~~~~~

We are creating all the time through our thoughts.

~~~~~~~~~

In the Old Testament Book of Jeremiah, we are told that the people of Judah had turned away from God and toward images of false gods instead. God sent the young prophet Jeremiah to warn the people of imminent destruction should they continue their worship of idols. (In other words, their mental equivalent of depravity and ugliness would foretell their downfall.) Jeremiah, sent to save the Judeans from themselves, was beaten and imprisoned for his message. Yet he obeyed his Creator, assuring the people of Judah that God was committed to loving them. "For I know the thoughts that I think toward you, says the Lord, thoughts of peace and not of evil, to give you a future and hope."

~~~~~~~~~

Whatever image our mind clings to will tend to
replicate itself in our real world. Unfortunately,
many of us create what we least want by
holding on to poor images.

~~~~~~~~~

When I read that passage, I think that God is calling all of us by name, saying, "These are My plans for you. Plans to prosper you. Plans to give you the life of your dreams." But God can't get through to us if we're worshiping idols. Maybe we're focusing on everything we think can go wrong, concocting pictures of doom or inadequacy. We think, "I really want relationships to work," but as with Mark, 90 percent of the time our mind rehashes all the ones that fell apart.

~~~~~~~~

God is calling all of us by name, saying, "These are My plans for you. Plans to prosper you. Plans to give you the life of your dreams."

~~~~~~~~

We begin by being more attentive to our thoughts, in order to notice what we are thinking. Without a new direction, our minds will continue to create exactly what they've always created. How can they not? We are thinking the thoughts we've always thought. In the last chapter, we discussed how our awareness of negative patterns is the first step toward designing the life for which we're intended. Creating a mental equivalent is the next step. Painting pictures in our mind of what we want serves as the foundation for greater living and greater relationships.

If we're accustomed to thinking a particular way, we can't expect to change our thinking overnight. The trend of our current thinking has a certain pull to it, born of sheer repetition. Like gravity, habitual thinking drops us back to ground level. To create a positive, vibrant mental equivalent, take your attention off what is and begin to explore what can be—which I know is easier said than done. Despite our best intentions, certain thoughts tend to short-circuit other ones, especially when strong emotions are involved.

You cannot eliminate limiting pictures from your mind through force or willpower. The only thing that works is to *substitute images*. Turn your attention, energy and enthusiasm to the very experience you desire to bring into being.

~~~~~~~~~~~

*You cannot eliminate limiting pictures from your mind
through force or willpower. The only thing that works
is to substitute images. Turn your attention,
energy and enthusiasm to the very experience you
desire to bring into being.*

~~~~~~~~~~~

Wonder whether or not you are equal to this task? Close your eyes for a moment and conjure this image: You are inside a beautifully detailed replica of the log cabin where Abraham Lincoln was born in Springfield, Illinois. Inside the dimly lit cabin, you will find the red bloomers Abe wore as a boy, the books he read and several of his early journals. You will also find a special display of the items found in his pocket the night he was assassinated. His right suit pocket held a five-dollar Confederate note, the pocketknife he had used as a child, a hand-kerchief with the initials A.L. stitched in the corner and a news-paper article about himself. Frayed in the corners, the article was heavily creased in several places, as if it had been unfolded, read and returned to his pocket again and again. The article, written by John Brite, a British statesman, said: "Abraham Lincoln is a brave and courageous leader." Perhaps Lincoln, despite being president of the United States, felt insecure at times and kept that clipping to remind himself of his potential and to help build his confidence.

Do you have a sense, even a glimpse of that cabin and its contents in your mind? Can you feel the brittle paper in your fingers? I am quite certain you have never visited this cabin, because it doesn't exist. The contents of Lincoln's pockets from the night he died in Ford's Theater are on display in the Smithsonian in Washington, D.C., but how many of you have been to that museum or recall that particular display? The point is, you can readily visualize something almost entirely outside your own experience.

We all have the power to substitute images and make a mental picture come to life. Ernest Holmes, author of *The Science of Mind,* believed, like Emmet Fox, that the manner in which we think determines our destiny. Holmes said, "Spirit is not bound by precedent," meaning that we don't have to limit ourselves to prior thoughts and experiences. When we have faith that the power of God will work through us, and are willing to do our part, we can create whatever good we choose.

If you could wave a magic wand and create the relationship of your dreams, how would it look? If you energize that picture with enthusiasm, you will eventually paint a clear scenario that has the potential to take form in the real world. When lesser pictures creep into your mind—and they will—close your eyes and substitute, again and again. This is a form of spiritual practice that pays huge dividends in every part of your life.

Here are some proven ways to hone your creative capacity:

UTILIZE ALL YOUR SENSES. Mental pictures are not limited to what we can see in our mind's eye. Hear your partner's voice. Touch his or her skin. Are the two of you strolling on the beach? Inhale the ocean air. Notice your sense of joy and aliveness as your pictures take form. The more feeling you bring to the ideal vision for the relationship, the more energy you'll have for bringing it into form. Be sure to create a positive, vivid mental equivalent that enlivens you, not an abstract demand that implies you've failed. "I should be nicer to my husband" will not get you very far.

Your ideal is not a relationship born out of duty or responsibility. If a vision of yourself as nurturing and caring feels burdensome, go back to the drawing table; something's out of place. The mental equivalent you want to create is a relationship that springs from genuine joy and desire. Remember the nervous elation you felt during those first phone calls of a fledgling romance? What about the way your heart leaped the first time you saw your own child? Let that same sense of joyful anticipation color your pictures, and you're moving them one step closer to reality.

ASK QUESTIONS. When Rembrandt's famous 1642 painting *The Night Watch* was restored and returned to the Rijks Museum in Amsterdam, the curators performed a simple, yet remarkable experiment in which they asked visitors to submit questions about the work. The painting depicts a group of city guardsmen, weapons at the ready, awaiting the command to fall in line. But in the center of the canvas, which is swirling with color, movement and light, stands a man dressed in yellow.

Some questions focused on issues that curators generally prefer to avoid, such as: How much did the painting cost? Has it ever been forged? Does the painting contain any mistakes? Others inquired about traditional artistic values. Why did Rembrandt choose that particular subject? Who were the people portrayed? What techniques did Rembrandt pioneer in this particular work? The curators prepared answers to over fifty queries.

In the room adjoining the gallery where *The Night Watch* was hung, museum staff papered the walls with these questions and answers. Visitors were obliged to pass through this room before entering the gallery.

~~~~~~~~

Within every question lies an adventure, an opportunity to experience our lives more deeply.

~~~~~~~~

The curious outcome was that the average length of time people spent viewing the painting increased fivefold: from six minutes to just over half an hour. Visitors alternated between reading questions and answers and looking at the painting. They said that the additional information not only enhanced their understanding of the work but motivated them to examine *The Night Watch* more thoroughly, to linger over small details that might have gone unnoticed, such as how the shadow of one color tones down the lightness of another. Seeing the painting from a completely new perspective, they looked more closely and remembered more. Like a series of magnets, the questions drew the visitors' thoughts to fresh ideas. They were truly curious about the painting and "got to know it" far better.

The word "question" originates from the Latin root *quaestio*, which means "to seek." Within every question lies an adventure, an opportunity to experience our lives more deeply. Now imagine a painting called *The Homecoming*, depicting you and your spouse greeting one another at the end of the workday. Are the characters in the piece embracing one another or reaching for the remote control? In the next gallery, there's a painting called *Homework*. Are parent and child sitting contentedly side by side or does the adult face show anger, and the child's frustration? Linger on your images and the other paintings that make up your world. Do they reflect the highest image you desire? If not, where are they lacking?

ACT ON THE IMAGE. The next step is vital. If your mental equivalent were possible, how might you act? Step into your picture and move about a little. We'll explore this subject further in later chapters, but for now, let's say you and your spouse have grown estranged. If your mental equivalent is of loving reciprocity, perhaps you'd stash a romantic card in his lunch bag, and feel throughout the day a special closeness for having extended love in an unexpected way.

What if you desire romance but are currently alone? You don't have to wait until Mr. or Mrs. Right materializes to attract more love into your life. Create a mental equivalent of yourself so loving and caring that you begin to pour that energy on the people in your life right now—friends, neighbors, children. I know that this may not be easy to do. Over my many years in the ministry, I have been saddened by those whose longing for a partner has left them feeling cheated and empty. I'm not denying their right to that pain, but pain won't make their lives any better. They focus almost exclusively on the absence of a companion, which manifests into . . . well, the absence of a companion. All the passion they keep bottled up inside begins to spoil, because it has nowhere to go. Passion spoiled turns bitter, and we all know how likely bitterness is to attract a mate.

I can't promise that loving others will guarantee your finding Mr. or Mrs. Right, but I do believe it will improve your chances. And loving others will definitely improve your life right now. Take that passion that is God's gift to you and lavish it on others. Think of yourself as being loved, because you are. God loves you, and probably many others do as well. Once you move from focusing on an absence of love to recognizing the abundance of love already within, you will stop postponing happiness. A life of loving is available now.

This process requires patience and diligence. Don't be disappointed if you try to step into your picture and trip over your original mental canvas now and then.

My friend, whom I'll call Gina, felt sorely neglected by her workaholic boyfriend, Ron. To salvage her dignity, she told herself that she needed to end the relationship, or at least berate him for not paying more attention to her. But that's not what she really wanted. Her heart's desire was for a loving, committed future together. She began working on her mental equivalent and saw that if their relationship were as she envisioned it, she would be sending him a loving e-mail.

"I just met with the designer for my new house," she wrote him, "and flashing on a pleasant memory, I told him that the shower had to be big enough for two . . . Maybe the bathtub, too.

What do you think?" Ron called a day later, leaving a distracted-sounding message about getting the right type of pipes for the tub.

Gina was devastated that her note hadn't set off sparks—"The last thing on my mind was plumbing"—but resolved not to stay hurt. Obviously, Ron was harried and had read her e-mail hastily. Visualizing hers as a truly loving relationship, she saw that one partner would show patience to another who might be distracted by work. She decided to allow Ron the time he needed and not push him about a commitment. In turn, Ron, who'd felt guilty for ignoring Gina, felt less pressured. And pressure was keeping him away as much as work. When he felt more relaxed, he began to share Gina's vision for their future, and eventually Ron tried out that bathtub.

Steve, a member of our congregation, had a harder time acting on his mental equivalent. Having grown up spoiled by wealth, he learned early on that money could buy his way out of any unpleasant situation. When work posed a challenge, he switched jobs. When relationships caused him stress, he ended them. Steve had three children from three different marriages and provided his offspring with good private schools, expensive toys and little else. His pocketbook was full, but his heart was bankrupt.

Steve came to a realization that he wanted something that money could not buy. He ached for the kind of relationship his friends had with their children. Steve had been raised in a household in which all investments were monetary instead of emotional. Now he vowed that he would begin to invest time and energy in his children. Steve began asking God for guidance. Soon, a picture of the kind of family relationship he desired filled his mind. The only trouble was, he didn't know how to activate the picture. It remained like a series of still photographs: his younger son rushing out the door to greet him, his daughter introducing him to her friends, his older boy asking for help with homework. But what would make his children look and act that way?

Every night, he would ask God to show him, but the message he received in return confounded him: "Keep looking." Keep looking? Steve had detailed his mental picture so finely, he could even see the dimples on his son's beaming face, responding to a loving father, a father who was ... what *was* he doing?

One day, while visiting a friend, he again noticed the closeness this man had with his children, and felt that familiar ache. But this time, Steve paid attention to precisely *how* the father communicated. He observed that his friend looked his kids in the eye, listened without interrupting and responded to questions without snapping or shouting, even if the answer seemed obvious. He noticed how his friend would hug his children or touch them lightly on the shoulder during conversation. "Keep looking." The words came back to him, and now Steve knew what they meant. Look closely at fathers he admired, and begin to duplicate their behavior.

When Steve attempted to connect with his children, he understood they might be leery of his motives and reject him. And they did shun him at first, perhaps following Steve's own model. In addition, Steve would still lose his temper at times and retreat when tension built. But he persisted, and the relationship with his children conceived in his mind was born into reality. He became the great father that he had longed in his heart to be and that his mind had imaged. Inside us is a literal artist-in-residence—God—and together, there is nothing beyond our capacity to create.

Thoughts That Transform

~ God has a great plan for me to live in love.

~ I no longer focus on flaws and loneliness. Instead, I use my creative power to mentally illustrate what I truly want in relationships.

~ With God's help, I have the power to bring my picture to life.

Practice

Discover the power of mental equivalents. Form a picture in your mind that describes what you want to create in a relationship. For a romantic relationship, perhaps you'll see a fire, two people holding hands, a book of poetry or one of you rubbing the other's feet. You might be walking on a beach or washing the dishes together. For a parent-child relationship, you might visualize yourself with your arm around him or her, reading a book together. Or maybe you're throwing around a football and laughing. Hold that image of yourself with the other person, filling in details each time your mind conjures the picture. Who is present? What are you doing? How is the other person looking at you? Cut a picture out of a magazine that reflects the relationship you would like to experience, and keep it somewhere private, but prominent, such as in your wallet or on your nightstand. Don't try to figure out all the details. But whenever you start to slip, refer back to your picture. Trust in the image, and trust that with God, all things are possible.

Next, invest emotional energy in the image. What feelings arise as you reflect on the picture? Do you have a feeling of belonging, trust and safety? Do you feel at home with the other person, no matter where you are? Can you be totally yourself, with no need to put on airs or act in a way designed to garner approval? With a child, do you feel protective? Do you feel trusted?

If this exercise sounds somewhat daunting, think about the last good movie you watched. Sitting there in the darkness, you became tense and fearful when the protagonist faced danger. A really good movie may cause you to scream, cry or cover your eyes. You feel the danger, romance or adventure as if it's really happening. You're looking at nothing but images on a screen, but you become lost in those images. So, too, can you lose yourself in the screen of your mind. In time, your movie will become a true life story.

THE ULTIMATE COMPANION

SPIRITUAL PRINCIPLE

Nearer than your own breath, right where you are,
God is. Just as you design relationships with
others, so, too, can you build a trusting, loving
companionship with God.

A boy and his father were out walking when they came across a large stone. The boy said to his father, "Do you think if I use all my strength, I can move this rock?" His father answered, "If you use all your strength, I am sure you can do it."

The boy began to push the rock. Exerting himself as much as he could, he pushed until sweat poured off his forehead, but the rock did not budge. Discouraged, the boy told his father, "You were wrong. I can't do it."

The father placed his arm around the boy's shoulder and said, "No, son. I was not wrong. You didn't use all your strength.

"You didn't ask me for help."

—Anonymous

7. How Prayer Is Answered

Most of the time, Sara didn't complain about the hand-me-downs—dresses frayed and faded from too many washings, pants gaping at the waist no matter how tightly she cinched them. No, knowing the state of the family finances, Sara took what she was given without question. Then those loafers arrived in her closet. Having already adorned the feet of two older sisters, the shoes that would see Sara through sixth grade were brown and dull as dirt, so unlike the slick sports shoes her classmates favored. More than anything, Sara wanted to fit in, but when she looked down at her feet, tears fell from her eyes, right onto the tarnished brass buckles of those big, ugly loafers.

Sara's mother had taught her a bedtime prayer, but the words meant little to the girl. She recited them each night by rote. Even at age eleven, however, she never neglected her act of devotion, on the assumption that God kept a checklist of slackers, and she didn't want a black mark by her name.

That night before the first day of sixth grade, she prayed with a fervor she hadn't known possible. She did not want to walk into the classroom with those clunky things on her feet. Reasoning that she'd dutifully recited her prayers all these years while asking little in return, she felt that God, in all fairness, ought to hold up His end of the bargain. "God," she asked, "please, please make my shoes different. If you've ever wanted to show yourself to me, show yourself to me this way. Give me shoes like everyone else's, so nobody will notice them and make fun of me."

When she opened her closet the following morning, there sat her loafers, brown and scuffed as ever. Sighing, Sara slipped them on and rode the bus to school, all the while thinking: "How can I walk in there with these shoes on? I'll just die if they laugh at me."

Slowly, an idea took hold. Perhaps she could keep her class-mates from even noticing her feet. She started talking to all the other children, asking them questions about their summer vaca-tions and their new teachers, hoping to engage them enough that they'd have no opportunity to look her anywhere but in the eye. During recess, Sara took charge of activities for the first time. She organized teams for playing tag, keeping everyone running and laughing, hoping her loafers would disappear in a blur of sneakers and patent leather. That afternoon, she went home pleased: "Nobody mentioned the shoes; not even once."

Knowing that her luck might soon run out, Sara went to bed that night once again praying for God to make her shoes differ-ent. Once again, she awakened to the sight of those ugly loafers in her closet. So she continued to strike up conversations with anyone who looked her way and to take charge of activities at re-cess. No child was left out, as Sara feared that an idle gaze might land on her feet.

By the end of the first week, one of her classmates ap-proached Sara and asked, "What happened to you last summer? You're different, really fun. You used to be okay, but not like this. Everybody just can't stop talking about Sara this year. They think you're really, really great."

As Sara lay in bed that night, she realized her prayer had indeed been answered. God had not made the shoes different; God had made Sara different. If Sara's loafers had miraculously turned into Nikes, her outlook might have brightened for a time. Eventually, however, the leather would have worn thin, as would have her belief. Instead, God guided her to a place that no pair of shoes could have taken her.

~~~~~~

As Sara lay in bed that night, she realized her prayer had indeed been answered. God had not made the shoes different; God had made Sara different.

~~~~~~

Think about the last time you prayed for something. Did you receive exactly what you wanted? Did your prayers go unanswered? Or, is it possible that God responded in such an unexpected way, you weren't even aware He had answered? Maybe what you had in mind for yourself paled in comparison to the good God intended. We may know intellectually that God always acts in accordance with our highest good, but we hesitate to believe that truth in our hearts. We don't necessarily trust our Creator to get things right.

Why should we? In the absence of a close, deep personal relationship, why should we trust God more than we would any other stranger?

Many of us say we believe in God; many of us feel that God is everywhere—except for right here. We stunt our own belief. We don't really think that we have access to infinite wisdom, to an infinite source of supply. We do not really think that given a tough circumstance, there is a Presence and there is a Power that is not only with us but for us. We do not reach out to access the spiritual bounty that is rightfully ours. Small thinking keeps us trapped in a small life, when what God offers each of us is a great one.

We can develop a connection with our Creator so that we know our prayers are indeed being answered. This relationship can be even more meaningful and accepting than the one we have with our closest friend. Suppose that you solicit your best friend for advice. If what your friend offered differed from your own plan, you'd probably still listen. You might even consider acting on the advice, simply because you trust that individual's wisdom and know that he or she has your well-being at heart. Imagine having such a relationship with God. As we read in Exodus, "And the Lord spoke unto Moses face to face as a man speaks to his friend."

The first step is to connect. Lawrence of Arabia used to tell a story about taking some of his chieftains from Arabia to Paris for peace talks. Strange objects on the bathroom walls amazed the chieftains. If they turned these objects clockwise, water poured out. The chieftains were flabbergasted that this precious gift of life could come spewing forth from a strange-looking knob.

When Lawrence of Arabia took the chieftains back home, he was greatly amused by the contents of their bags. For tucked amid the robes and sandals were the faucets and handles his men had pried loose from the hotel bathrooms. They mistakenly believed that these bits of porcelain and brass were the source of the water and that if they just affixed them to their tents, they would never want for water again.

We may chuckle, because we know that water will not flow from a faucet that is not connected to its source. Yet we can be just as quick to want answers from God without first establishing contact. Often, new members of our church will tell me that they don't know how to talk to God. I tell them that there's a "getting to know you" phase. Maybe you don't know how to communicate, I tell them, but you're willing to learn, and your willingness is all that's required. In that initial phase, you stop demanding answers and start to realize that God is already providing guidance that you may not yet recognize. In this early phase, you focus on a willingness to develop the relationship more than on receiving answers, and recognizing that everywhere you see life, is evidence of God's Presence.

Many of us haven't connected because we're stuck in a fifth-grade image of God. We never let our image of God grow up. As children, most of us pictured God as a man in the sky. We may have believed God to be either punishing or kindly, but most likely we believed that God was tuned in to the minutiae of our life, an airborne Santa in more formal attire, sitting on a cloud deciding who's naughty and nice. Young children in particular tend to see themselves as the center of the universe, so naturally, when kids say their prayers at night, God listens. As a little girl, I would add a postscript to my nightly amens, saying, "This is Mary talking, God," because God knew me by name.

Then disillusionment sets in. If we had a sense of God's being nearby, most of us lose it as we grow up. We discover injustice, poverty and our own seeming limitations. Perhaps God isn't as all-powerful as we once imagined, and neither are we. So we come to reject the notion of the Big-Man-in-the-Sky, and along with it, the belief that God cares for and communicates with us individually.

Many people who walk through the doors of the church I serve left organized religion behind years earlier. Some became disillusioned because they felt their church had preached rhetoric and dogma but had not really brought them closer to God. Jeannie told me she left the church she grew up in when she could no longer believe in a God who would send millions of people to hell because they didn't believe the way her church members did. Did God listen only to the prayers of a select few? she wondered. George told me he left church as a teen when he couldn't reconcile the message of the pulpit with the behavior of the congregation. If love was the message, why did gossip, bickering and backstabbing run rampant in his church? Tom stopped praying after he asked God to heal his brother of cancer and his brother died. Sharon stopped talking with God after her prayers for a life companion went unanswered.

Yet something in us all deeply yearns for spirituality, and these folks had come to the Living Enrichment Center to try to either renew their relationship with God or to forge one for the first time. Our longing for God may get covered or disguised, but it never goes away. And neither does God's longing for us.

~~~~~~~

Our longing for God may get covered or disguised, but it never goes away. And neither does God's longing for us.

~~~~~~~

The intimate God of our early childhood—we talk, God listens; God talks, we listen—can exist for us on an adult level, and can mature into the most important relationship of our life. We can come to know God as an all-pervasive Presence who is available to us individually and personally and who has never stopped caring for us, no matter how hard we try to operate on our own.

My young stepson, Matthew, used to love what I call The Claw, that tempting machine at supermarkets and video arcades that will dispense a stuffed animal to the lucky winner. You drop in a quarter and manipulate a lever that looks like a metal claw, trying to grab one of the enticing little puppies or bunnies jumbled together at the bottom of a glass case.

Every week, Matthew would convert his allowance to quarters and beg to accompany me to the supermarket. He'd run up to the machine and speak nicely to it, giving it a little friendly pat for luck. And then he'd deposit his quarter and furrow his brow in concentration as he tried to pluck a prize in the allotted time. More often than not, the claw grabbed nothing but air, so he tried again and again, until his stash of quarters was depleted. On those rare occasions he won a stuffed animal, he'd bring it to the dinner table for an entire week and then forget about it. Most of the time, however, he won nothing, so he'd kick the machine and walk away.

Some of us treat God like The Claw. We want our Creator to be a divine vending machine that dispenses the toys we desire. Receiving fills us with happiness, but walking away empty-handed leaves us feeling cheated, which raises the question: Do we love God or do we merely love what we think God can give us? Do we want the toys, or do we want the relationship? What kind of prayer tries to manipulate God for personal benefit? Whether we seek to acquire or heal, we're presupposing that a relationship with God means God will fulfill our wants, and that kind of selfish thinking runs contrary to the true nature of what an authentic relationship with God means.

All of us have had relationships with people we call users. They call us when their car breaks down and they need transportation; they call us to fix a leaky faucet or to complain about their boss or to borrow money. But their infrequent thanks have a perfunctory ring and they rarely offer anything in return or inquire about our own lives. You may have noticed, too, that these folks tend to reject any assistance or ideas you may offer that aren't precisely what they've requested. The best help is often dismissed out of hand. And do these people ever call just to say hello?

So imagine what it's like when we only approach God to ask for what we want. Even if we get exactly what we're after, we always wind up feeling as if something's still missing, because our soul longs for a relationship with God, not a quick fix.

Another reason we may seek help is because we're in pain and want it to stop. In the midst of a divorce, when diagnosed with a serious illness or unexpectedly unemployed, we're in such agony that nothing else has worked and so finally we try God. There's nothing wrong with initiating a relationship in crisis. It's what happens after the pain recedes that matters. Maybe we recover and begin to drift again. We check in with God from time to time, which is fine but won't build the kind of relationship for which our soul is longing.

We pray at times when we feel separate from God but we don't always pray in such a way that we develop an ongoing partnership. How can we do that?

As in any other relationship, we communicate about what's important to us and learn to trust over time. We cannot know in advance how the relationship will turn out, but by making ourselves available, by continually forging deeper levels of connection, we prepare to receive grace however God manifests in our life. Prayer is how we get to know God better. Prayer is not a get-on-your-knees begging and pleading or a mindless recitation of words, but a kind of thinking and feeling. Prayer is communing and communicating with God.

As in any other relationship, we communicate about what's important to us and learn to trust over time.

Certainly, we can ask God for help with what we want. In the context of any trusting, give-and-take relationship, requests are perfectly natural. We ask friends for favors all the time. But those favors are only one part of the relationship.

Practice remembering God. Practice thinking in a way that God is never really absent from your thoughts. Practice remembering that your present circumstances are not insurmountable, because God is greater than your history and greater than any challenge you may be facing. Jesus said, ". . . when you pray, go into your room and when you have shut your door, pray to your Father who is in the secret place . . ." He didn't mean that you have to go off to some private sanctuary; he meant go inside yourself. So when we want to get close to God, when we want to come to a deeper awareness of who we really are, and what to do, we go within. We begin to shift our thinking higher to remember God. While we cannot control people, places, circumstances or things, we can lift our perspective through prayer.

~~~~~~~

*Practice remembering God. Practice thinking in a way
that God is never really absent from your thoughts.*

~~~~~~~

Prayer is our link to our Creator, a way to lift thoughts and feelings into synchrony with that still, small voice, the voice for God. Some of us hear the word "prayer" and think, "I've got to sit and repeat something or meditate twenty minutes in the afternoon." Authentic prayer is simply a thought of truth that when held long enough and strongly enough evokes in us a felt shift. We learn to trust something greater than our own intellect.

The solution to the problems before us isn't more money or fewer difficult people in our lives, because the only real problem is disconnection from God. Solutions come as we connect with a higher level of thinking and knowing. Albert Einstein said: "The significant problems we face cannot be solved at the level of thinking that created them." When we lift ourselves in connection with God, an entirely new realm of thought becomes available to us. If we go back and acknowledge God's presence and power in the midst of a troubling circumstance, ideas and insight come that lead toward resolution.

The Apostle Paul said, "Pray unceasingly." He meant stay connected. We really can work with our thoughts so that we continually remind ourselves of the One Presence and Power, always with us and for us. The experience of God's presence is only a thought away. As our relationship deepens, we find a growing trust in God. We find that whenever we call on the Presence, God is there. We do not have to feel alone. We do not have to ask ourselves, "Is there anyone who cares?" because we know that our Creator always cares. As we learn to connect consciously with God, we begin to experience a relationship that includes comfort and a deep sense of well-being, a feeling of companionship, guidance, protection and provision.

In rock climbing, there is a step called a "commitment move." You're tied to the ropes, and there's a moment you have to let go of solid ground to move to the next higher place. It's a scary step. You must trust what you're tied to more than what you're standing on.

Jesus offers the same lesson: What you're tied to is so much greater than the little bit you're standing on—or in. The clunky loafers on your feet aren't holding you back. The One to whom you're connected is far greater than any circumstance. If you willingly step out, motivated by something grander than getting what you want or relief from pain, then you keep in the practice of growing a relationship with God even in the good times. You don't look to God as a servant, to fetch and fix. You look to God as partner in the most precious and profound relationship in your life.

~~~~~~

THOUGHTS THAT TRANSFORM

~ God always answers my prayers, even when I'm unaware of the response.

~ I can have a relationship with God that is even closer than the one I have with my best friend.

~ The greatest commitment move I can make is choosing to connect with God.

~ Prayer doesn't change others—it changes me.

PRACTICE

Begin each morning by asking God: What would You have me do today? Then listen for an impulse, idea or directive. God will direct you to settle a dispute, call a friend in need, articulate your heart's desire—some action to align you with your divine nature, which is love.

Look for opportunities for God to show up. As you practice seeing God in every person you encounter, you may also begin to notice that flowers in bloom have turned more vibrant, that the leaves in the trees are a richer shade of green. Opening to God's presence is like emerging from a dark closet into daylight. Your whole world is more expansive and beautiful.

Communicate with God in a new way. Choose a time free of interruptions, when you can relax and savor the silence. Our minds all contain sediment that prevents us from seeing clearly. As we take a few minutes each day to sit in silence, we can let the unwanted static settle. We can clarify our thoughts. We find God in silence. The absence of silence prevents authentic listening. Silence is part of the way we carve a deeper place in ourselves where the roots of awareness can grow, so that when we're nudged, we say Yes! That's a great idea, and we can choose to give room for it in the soil of our life. We can let that idea grow so its roots have some depth. Then, when the winds come or change occurs, we remain strong, and a precious new idea has a chance to grow. As Confucius said, "Those who would cultivate an entire empire must first cultivate themselves by finding that still space that opens the door to all knowledge."

Ask for insight. Instead of praying that God make someone else or an unpleasant circumstance change, ask that you be the one who is changed. Ask to see a person or situation from a higher perspective. Then be willing to try on a new way of seeing.

8. SIGNS AND SIGNALS

Lilly wanted to find Mr. Right. She had come to a number of retreats at our church, and I knew how much she longed to find a partner. She had married young, divorced and raised two children on her own. Now, she said, she was ready for the love of her life.

She told me that she had envisioned a relationship with a partner who was kind, trustworthy and had a great sense of humor. Ideally, he would enjoy gourmet cooking and Woody Allen movies. Then, as it happened, Lilly met someone who fulfilled every criteria, except for one: The man in question was ten years her junior.

"I guess I left out that part about the age," she told me.

Following her heart, Lilly became involved with this man nevertheless, and the relationship blossomed. As the two grew more serious, she began holding heated arguments with herself: "I can't do this. He's younger than I am." Then she would counter, "Well, why can't I? How come men can fall in love with a younger woman, but if the guy's younger, then I feel like 'Oh, what's going to happen in ten years? I'll be an old crow.'" Lilly really cared about this man and began coating her skin with alpha hydroxy, streaking her graying hair blond and consulting a dermatologist about collagen implants. Maybe she could outfox Mother Nature.

Then one day she caught her reflection in the mirror. "I look pretty good," she said to herself. "I'm a good-looking, middle-aged woman. But no matter what I do, I'm still going to be ten years older than him.

"God," she asked, "what should I do? I love this man, but the age difference scares me to death. He may want children, and I've already had mine. A few years from now, he'll still look young, and I'll have wrinkles. He may not want me anymore. And God, I couldn't bear to lose him then. I don't want to lose him now, but I couldn't bear it then. Please help me to find an answer."

A few weeks later, Lilly drove to our Sunday services early, having spent a restless night fretting over her relationship. Normally, as she told me later, she rides in silence because she likes to prepare herself to fully absorb the message. But this Sunday, she felt a nudge so sharp it felt almost like a jab. The nudge told her, "Turn on the radio."

She thought, "No, I never listen to the radio on Sunday mornings," but the nudge grew stronger still.

"Turn on the radio."

Lilly flicked the dial to the Public Broadcasting Station. A special program on Brahms was on. "Ah," she thought. "I love Brahms. Maybe this was a message from God to stop worrying, to just relax and enjoy the music."

After the conclusion of a sonata, the narrator spoke of the influences on Brahms's creativity. At age fifty-five, he noted, the composer had fallen in love with a woman who had inspired him to write some of his most passionate music. The narrator went on to add a little-known fact, that the musician's great love was fifteen years his senior. The woman responsible for igniting Brahms's romantic compositions was seventy years old.

Now Lilly knew why she'd been nudged to turn on the radio that morning. "Thank you, God, for this message!" she said aloud. The music continued to play itself in her mind, and each time she heard not just the notes, but the love that Brahms had rendered immortal. The crow's-feet that had so worried her faded into insignificant lines that just scratched the surface. Lilly knew that what she had to offer was far deeper. Six months later, she and her partner were married.

God communicates with us in powerfully subtle ways, even through the glorious notes of a sonata. You may find unexpected messages in a line from a movie or television program. You may be in a mall and overhear a snippet of conversation that speaks directly to you. Once you pay attention, your awareness of God's Presence magnifies. You begin to feel loved and nurtured and provided for in a way that seems inconceivable if your mind is fixed on nothing but the trouble at hand.

God is nudging you right now, offering a direction for your life where fulfillment and joy abound. God may ask you to take a difficult step. The nudge may be: "You need to let that resentment go," or "You need to take a step out of the comfort that's keeping you confined." It may be that you need to tell the truth about something you've kept hidden from a loved one.

To increase awareness of God's nudges, we can establish a pattern of attentiveness. No one begins by paying attention all the time. Consider those times when you lose focus, oblivious to your environment or the task before you.

To increase awareness of God's nudges, we can
establish a pattern of attentiveness.

Have you ever been driving along a freeway and suddenly realize that you haven't been aware of your surroundings for the past five miles? You might have asked yourself: "Did I miss my exit?" When we're not attending to the task of driving, it's as if we're asleep at the wheel. Similarly, we can be asleep to the Presence of God. That Presence is right here, but if we're unaware, we miss the road we intended to take.

I remember tucking in my stepson one night, anxious to return to a mystery I'd been reading. Kissing his forehead, I said, "Good night, Matthew," to which he replied: "My tummy feels a little funny."

"Oh, I'm sorry, but I'm sure it will be all right, sweetie. Let's try this," I responded. Then, holding my hand over his stomach, I recited a quick little prayer and headed off to bed with my book.

A few hours later, I heard Matthew burst out of his bedroom and run frantically down the hall, followed by the unmistakable eruptions recognized by parents the world over. Matthew's dad desperately pretended to be asleep, but I eventually roused Ed for what I knew would be a two-person cleanup job.

I took a message from that night: Pay attention to the little nudges—the tummy aches and so on—or you may have a real mess on your hands. If we can ignore something as overt as nausea, how can we possibly become attuned to our Creator's more subtle messages? The great news is, the more we attend to our inner guidance, the more alive we feel, and the more sensitive we become to God's Presence.

Perhaps some of you are asking: How do we recognize guidance when it comes? How do we distinguish God's nudge from all the other voices clamoring for attention? In fact, we all have an inner knowing that indicates when something merits our attention. Consider those times when you're watching TV, only half-engaged, and all of a sudden a voice comes on: "We interrupt this broadcast for an important announcement." Or you're flying in an airplane, engrossed in a book, and the plane hits an air pocket, dropping two hundred feet. That gets your attention. Then you hear a voice: "Ladies and gentlemen, this is the captain . . ." Now you're sitting up straight, straining to hear every word.

God, too, interrupts the daily broadcast of our lives with important bulletins. We might be at work, dining, watching television or lifting weights and receive the nudge: "We interrupt this scheduled program to give you an important announcement. You need to be a little more compassionate. Why don't you forgive that old resentment? Why don't you go help out at the kids' school?"

A friend of mine was riding the scheduled ferry from Victoria, British Columbia, to the mainland in Port Angeles, Washington. About halfway across Puget Sound, some passengers spotted a family of whales frolicking in the distance. The ferry operator, hearing the commotion, announced the whale sighting and much to the passengers' surprise, promptly veered off course. Perhaps one hundred yards shy of the whales, he cut the motor, giving those on board a close-up look at these stunning mammals. There the ferry remained, bobbing quietly in the surf, until the whales disappeared from sight. The ferry docked more than a half hour past its scheduled arrival, but nobody complained. My friend, who had been on vacation, said this unexpected event was the highlight of her trip.

If we don't allow God's interruptions, we're going to miss out on some of the really big things in life. We need to allow for a change in plans. Many of us listen for God's guidance when we pray. Maybe we've set aside time in the morning or evening to check in with God or offer gratitude. These are critical practices in getting to know God better. We do need to schedule time with God. But let us not forget that God does not limit Spirit's calendar to our itinerary.

God is with us all day long and will tap us on the shoulder whenever the time is right as if to say, "Excuse me, why don't you stop whatever you're doing and pay attention. This message is for you, and it's an important one."

~~~~~~

If we don't allow God's interruptions, we're going to
miss out on some of the really big things in life.
We need to allow for a change in plans.

~~~~~~

I had several years of spiritual study under my belt before I came to understand this concept. Then one day, it hit me: *"This is the practice."* It isn't just about the meditation in the morning and at night. Spiritual practice means remembering God all day long, because when I'm in contact, I feel the nudges; I allow the interruptions. And when I disconnect, when resentments build or I snap at someone or judge harshly, I'm numb to the nudges. I cling to my plan, forgetting that I am part of a much grander one.

~~~~~~

Spiritual practice means remembering God all day
long, because when I'm in contact, I feel the nudges;
I allow the interruptions. And when I disconnect, when
resentments build or I snap at someone or judge
harshly, I'm numb to the nudges. I cling to my plan,
forgetting that I am part of a much grander one.

~~~~~~

As your relationship with God matures, you learn to discern God's nudges and trust the wisdom contained in the interruptions. My friend Robert was a spy with the French Resistance during World War II who used the alias "Mr. Parizot." His was a dangerous life, never more so than the day the Nazis stormed his Paris office in the city's information center. Robert was sitting at his desk on the fourth floor when his secretary ran in, panicked, saying, "The Gestapo is downstairs! And they're asking for Parizot!"

Terrified, Robert grabbed his briefcase, raced upstairs to the attic and crouched hidden in a corner. The Nazis would tear this building apart, brick by brick, and they would find him. But it was not death he feared. He feared the way death would come, the method the Nazis would use to end his life.

In that moment of terror, when he sat shuddering in a corner, fearing that God had abandoned him, an idea popped into his mind. He had been reading how we can change our reality by changing our thoughts, and what he'd learned began to fill his mind: *God is always available. God is not holding back from me; I hold back from God. And the shift has to happen in me.*

His life had been interrupted in the most dramatic way possible, but if God was always present, then God would guide him here as well.

There's another way to see this, but how?

What if . . . what if instead of seeing this as terrifying and being frozen in fear, I could think something else: I could think . . . I could think . . . "This is a thrilling adventure."

There, tucked in his corner, Robert nearly laughed out loud. How could he think of capture by the sadistic Gestapo as a thrilling adventure? *They're going to kill me!* But he knew that if he didn't make a shift, he would remain frozen. Yet, he felt God nudging him to action. *If this were a thrilling adventure, what would I do? If this were a thrilling adventure, if this were a movie, what would I do?*

I wouldn't hide, because they would expect me to hide and they would find me. What's the last thing they're going to expect me to do? And he felt another nudge.

The last thing the Nazis would expect is for me to walk out the front door.

So Robert slicked back his hair, smoothed his jacket and casually lit a cigarette. Down he trotted with his briefcase to the fourth floor, where his secretary simply gaped at him.

"What's going on here?" he demanded loudly, gesturing at the gun-toting Nazi officers.

"They're looking for a Mr. Parizot," she said, playing along.

Robert then said, "Parizot? I just saw him go out the back door!" And *whew!* The Nazis flew out the back, and the spy who called himself Parizot went out the front, hopped on his bike and made his escape.

The possibility for escape always existed, but my friend Robert Muller, who would later become assistant secretary-general of the United Nations, would never have seen an opportunity without opening to a nudge from God. Robert, who wrote *2,000 Ideas and Dreams for a Better World,* had to tune in to a different message than his fear, trusting that God could guide him. Robert was receptive to a change in plan. He recognized the hand of God and followed in the direction he was led.

Thoughts That Transform

~ I really have a trustworthy God, but I don't find that out unless I deliberately attune to divine nudges, signs and signals.

~ I welcome God's interruption, knowing Spirit has a plan more important than my own agenda.

~ I must wake up to my life. I do not want to risk losing a single precious moment.

Practice

To discern God's nudges from the cacophony of lesser signals, establish a pattern of attentiveness. Begin each morning by setting your intention to remember God and attend to divine nudges. Do this before you even get out of bed. I've found that if I've postponed my initial greeting to God until after I've brushed my teeth or made that critical business call, the next thing I know, I've downed a slice of toast and some coffee and am bolting out the door to work. The entire day, I have the nagging sense I've missed or lost something. On those rare mornings I miss spending a moment or two with my husband, I'm thrown off-kilter. I want to share a good-bye kiss and the reminder that we love one another. We need even more that same exchange of love with our Source.

If you just get up and rush out the door, there's no time to consciously connect with your Creator, no base of connection from which you can spend your day. You slow morning people, who love the "reset" button on your alarm clocks, should try lingering in bed awake instead of dozing those extra few minutes. Silently or aloud, offer a greeting or affirmation. Often I'll say, "God, I want to be present to You today. I want to do my part. I promise to attend to any nudge I feel from You today. I know You are with me, always, and for that I am grateful."

Throughout the day, have regular moments during which you pause and tell yourself: "There's a Presence and a Power with me and for me. It's greater than anything around me. If I remember to remember that God is always with me, then how can I not feel God in the sway of the branches on the trees, in the meals I prepare for my family, every place I go and in everyone I meet?" Over time, inner communion grows into a companionship that can never be broken.

Before you go to bed each night, listen to the voice of God's wisdom. If there's any unfinished business of the day, deal with it. Unfinished business, hurts, disappointments, grudges become like static in the mind that interferes with God's otherwise clear signal. Deal with whatever needs to be discarded, forgiven or released from the day and tune in to God's presence.

The last thing at night, say something to the effect

of: "Thank you for this day. Speak to me in my dreams. I'm available and receptive." I know that if I set my intention morning and night and rehearse lines that help keep me tuned in, then I am aware of the nudges more often, I feel the Presence more powerfully. God can speak to you in a more powerful way if you pay attention.

9. Strong Enough to Weather Any Storm

Fulfilling my dream of buying a house made me so giddy with excitement that I walked around touching the walls, the white carpets, even the smooth porcelain of the toilets, announcing to everyone within earshot, "I'm a home owner! I'm a home owner!" Contrary to what my behavior might indicate, I was not a young, wide-eyed newlywed. When I signed mortgage papers for the first time, I was forty-five years old, a mother of four, a stepmom of two and a grandmother of one.

My first husband and I had married young and rented, then moved into a farm owned by his family. There we remained for seventeen years. The place never felt like my own, as I always felt compelled to consult my mother-in-law before making any decorating decisions.

Shortly after Ed and I married, we found our dream home in a suburb of Portland. The three-story traditional home sat atop a hill, overlooking the city. It was beautiful. It was also out of our price range, so we arranged a lease option that allowed us to put a portion of our rent toward the down payment should we ever be able to purchase the house. When we finally did sign those mortgage papers two years later, I felt almost like I had given birth after a twenty-four-month gestation. The home was my new baby, and I loved it with all my heart. Ed teased me because he had owned homes before, so being a property owner was not such a big deal for him. But it was a tremendously big deal for me.

"God has surely blessed the Morrisseys," I thought every time I looked at the moldings or cleaned the already-gleaming wood floors. "We're so fortunate," I told myself.

~~~~~~~~

"We're so fortunate," I told myself.

~~~~~~~~

Then it started raining.

Given its frequent rainfall, Oregon is the butt of many a fair-weather joke, and we Oregonians know how to cope. But despite our stalwart Northwest spirit, nothing could have prepared us for February 1996, when we were visited by a flood of biblical proportions. Chunks of the state literally slipped underwater. Small towns in particular were devastated. When the front page of *The Oregonian* pictured a boat bobbling down a small-town Main Street, I thanked God that we were safe on our hilltop.

~~~~~~~~

Then it started raining.

~~~~~~~~

One night, however, the wind shook the house and water splashed the siding so hard that I dreamed I was trapped on a rowboat in a tidal wave. Waking up was a relief, until I saw my husband's face. He had gone outside for the newspaper and returned looking soaked and shocked.

"The neighbors are moving out," he announced. "Their house is slipping down the hill."

"Oh, no!"

"And that's not all. Their house is pulling a portion of the hill with it."

"What portion would that be?" I asked, uncertain if I wanted an answer.

"The part of the hill that is underneath our house. There's police outside, and they're saying we have to evacuate."

"When?" I asked.

"Right now. We're losing our foundation. They think our house is falling down the hill, too. We better get dressed."

The drenching rains had acted like solvent, separating the house from its foundation. Numbly, I ran through the house, frantically filling suitcases with clothing, photo albums and other mementos from the kids' childhood. We hastily moved into a hotel, but as soon as I had a moment to think, I realized I needed to return home. The church had just begun a ten-day retreat, with visitors from all over the world, and I'd only packed clothing for two days.

Yellow crime-scene tape reading "Do not cross" stretched across the front of my dream house. Here I had waited forty-five years for a place to call my own and thirty days after closing, my home had been declared off-limits. I felt angry, cheated and profoundly sad. I remember thinking: "Oh great, from home owner to homeless. Move to the base of a valley in a wet climate, and you're inviting trouble. But how can you be flooded when you live on *top* of a hill? How dare nature treat me this way!"

Mother Nature lay beyond my control, but I could certainly defy the police. Since the officers had left the scene, I rushed inside, determined to have what might well be one last look at my beloved home.

The utility companies had turned off the electricity and water. The house, cold and dark in the middle of the afternoon, felt like a tomb. My footsteps echoed in the silence. I had the strange sensation I often felt when conducting a funeral, that the body in the casket before me was only a shell for the human spirit. No matter the stillness, the essence of what made that person unique lived on. The true essence of what made this structure a home was not the walls or the carpeting, but the people who shared it.

As I walked through the darkened halls, a scripture from the

Gospel of Matthew came to mind. "And the rain descended, and the floods came, and the winds blew, and burst against that house; and yet it did not fall, for it had been founded upon rock.

"And everyone who hears these words of Mine and does not act upon them, will be like a foolish man, who built his house upon the sand.

"And the rain descended, and the floods came, and the winds blew, and burst against that house; and it fell, and great was its fall."

These words echoed not only in my mind, but in my heart, and I knew that I had placed my security on a foundation that wasn't strong enough. My security doesn't lie in the structure of stone and wood, but in the strength of my relationship with God. When you invite God into your true home, nothing of value can ever be destroyed.

~~~~~~~~~

My security doesn't lie in the structure of stone and wood, but in the strength of my relationship with God.

~~~~~~~~~

As soon as I remembered this truth, my experience of this whole "disaster" began to change. I walked along the upstairs hallway that led to the bedrooms of the children. Those kids were all safe in a hotel with Ed. Suddenly, I felt overwhelming gratitude at God's goodness. Within me was a home that couldn't be washed away by rain. The recognition came that I'd found a wonderful home with God long before I had a house with my name on it.

When we'd signed those mortgage papers, I'd been profoundly grateful. I'd thanked God for the opportunity to own my own home. Such gratitude matters, but it is not the sort that carved my soul or deepened my relationship with God. Most of us feel grateful easily enough in good times. It's as if we invite God into our home as a guest, when everything is cleaned and polished and prepared for the best. We call on God for special occasions. But what if we invite God to share every moment with us, good and bad?

All relationships work this way, although we often forget. In a new relationship, we want the other person to see us at our best, often going to great lengths to hide our flaws and foibles. We want to make a good impression. Yet the relationship doesn't really start to mature until we allow the other person to share in our everyday life, to let that person support us when we're at our worst.

Those bad times do come. We all know tough circumstances. It is tough when the doctor delivers a bad diagnosis or when your child cannot seem to learn. It is tough when a relationship with a loved one ends. It is tough when we age and our bodies don't work the way they once did. Yet no matter how dire the circumstances, we can call on a loved one for help. Similarly, we can call on God.

That doesn't mean we don't become angry, disappointed or sad over misfortune, but in that storm of emotions, we can create a small, peaceful sanctuary within. In the midst of a house falling off a hill, in the midst of the soup underneath that I'd thought was solid, a great and wondrous thing happened. I saw that relationship with God would outlast beams and siding. The connection I felt with my Creator protected me, shielded me from the elements in a way no four walls ever could.

〜〜〜〜〜

I saw that relationship with God would outlast beams
and siding. The connection I felt with my Creator
protected me, shielded me from the elements in
a way no four walls ever could.

〜〜〜〜〜

Jesus says to us that we can build a house that will sustain any flood, any difficulty. Does that mean that the wind will not come? No. Does it mean a storm will not wash my house down the hill? No. Does it mean the disaster you dread most may not occur? No. But it means that in the midst of your disaster—the breakup of a marriage, the illness of a child—your relationship with God can remain solid and protect you. God's love is bigger than a flood. Bigger than wind. Bigger than divorce. Bigger than death. By inviting God to take up permanent residence in our home, we create a foundation stronger than anything life might send our way.

Even in the midst of crisis, there's a statement that I know is absolutely true: "God is good all the time." God is good not just when every little thing goes my way or when I happen to approve of what is happening. God is the source of all goodness and is present all the time. Even when my house is slipping off the hill, God is good. This life is all about relationship, with God, self and others.

As my friend Dr. Michael Beckwith says, "Stop telling God about your big problems and start telling your problems about your big God."

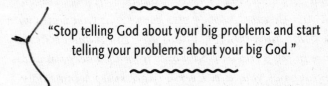

"Stop telling God about your big problems and start telling your problems about your big God."

It took two years and more money than I care to count to repair all the damage, but our house did survive. After excavating, workers drove twenty-six-foot steel pilings into the ground, anchoring them to the earth and to the house's foundation; the house was literally anchored to bedrock. Ed said: "The whole hill could fall away now, and our home isn't going anywhere."

Then we looked at each other and smiled, because we both knew those words referred to much more than just our physical house. We have an awesome God and a relationship stronger than any rain that falls. Nobody welcomes a flood, but with God as a permanent resident in your home, what is most important can never be washed away.

~~~~~~

THOUGHTS THAT TRANSFORM

~ I'm accustomed to offering thanks to God when everything goes well. But our relationship strengthens if I can learn to be grateful during the bad times as well. In the midst of any tempest, I can create a small, peaceful sanctuary within.

~ God is good, all the time.

~ I can invite God into my home at any time. I don't have to wait for a special occasion.

PRACTICE

Spend one day with God. This is absolutely private between you and your Creator. Nobody else knows that God walks with you as a companion throughout this day. But it makes all the difference in the world as God moves from the background to the foreground of your life. Everyday activities become holy experiences.

Walk through the day in your mind. Ask God for help in all that you anticipate—the meetings, the confrontations with your children or spouse, any encounters you may have. Yes, God is present anyway, but by formally issuing that invitation, you're much more likely to remember and partner with your Creator.

At some point in the day, you're going to shower. Bathing can be a sacrament just like baptism. This can be a time to not only become physically clean, but to allow your thoughts to become clean with God. As part of your spiritual practice, you clean your feet and are reminded that where you stand this day is holy ground. You wash your hands and think about the way that you touch others. You brush your teeth and resolve to speak in ways that are pure.

Imagine dining with God at the table. When eating in the presence of God, your mealtime ritual differs. You are less likely to rush. You are less likely to turn on the television and more likely to communicate with those close to you. You are less likely to excuse yourself from the table to take a phone call. You can connect and commune over a meal.

Imagine driving with God in the car. I know, this may sound strange. But commuting is often a time people are distanced from their higher mind. Anger and frustrations surface in traffic. Should you imagine God next to you, however, those many hours spent on the road, in a subway, even on a crowded bus, no longer plague you. If you commute by car, you may be less likely to cut off other drivers or curse at them under your breath. Your body no longer tenses at delays and congestion. Think of how you sometimes greet your loved ones after a rough commute. How differently might you greet them after commuting with God in the car?

With God your companion at every juncture, you notice that you are not alone. You begin to see people differently. You notice that who you eat with and how you eat changes. What you do with your money changes. Your whole life takes on new meaning and purpose. And when the rains fall, as they inevitably do, you can find true solace in God's presence.

You really can have one day with God. And that will give you the ability to have one more day with God. And then another.

THE POWER OF UNREASONABLE GIVING

SPIRITUAL PRINCIPLE

You are a child of God, who is the unconditional giver of life itself. By learning to give without keeping score, you enrich your relationship with God, with others and with yourself. It is in the act of giving that you truly receive.

When you discover the wonder of giving, you will wonder how you could have lived so long in any other way. It is the key that opens the door to every good thing in your life. It opens the door to the good you have been seeking and gives life every new dimension. It gives you the feeling and the knowing that truly you live in an abundant and plentiful universe and it is yours. It can be one of the greatest discoveries of your life. When you become a committed giver, you can no more go back to the old way of living than you can go back to prehistoric times.

—NORMAN VINCENT PEALE

10. PHILANTHROPY OF THE SOUL

In the movie *As Good as It Gets*, Jack Nicholson plays an aging fussbudget with the social skills of a goat who falls for a waitress played by Helen Hunt. As she joins him for dinner on their first date, he says he can't believe the maitre d' would treat *him* so shabbily after letting Hunt's character into the restaurant in what "looks like a housedress."

On the verge of storming out, Helen Hunt's character tersely tells him, "I need a compliment now, and make it good."

Jack Nicholson launches into the story of his problem-plagued life. Working up to the present, he rambles on about recent changes he's made, including caring for his neighbor's dog and taking medicine for his manic-depressive disorder. With just a trace of sarcasm in her voice, Helen Hunt cuts him off: "What I don't understand is how this is a compliment about *me*."

He pauses and says: "You make me want to be a better man."

Looking at him as she never has before, she says: "That may be the best compliment anyone has ever paid me."

Think for a moment: Has someone enriched your life such that you strive to be a better person? What is the best compliment anyone has ever paid you? What life-changing compliment have you given someone else?

Proverbs tells us: "A cheerful face is like medicine to the weary soul." I believe that we all have, or have the potential to have, relationships that restore and renew us. If your life already contains such generous individuals, acknowledge them. Consider putting down this book and writing them a thank-you note right now.

By contrast, if you're thinking, "On this planet?" or "Nobody cares for me that way," read on.

If you lack inspiring friends and loved ones, take a close look—at you. When we feel needy and empty, we can easily see only what others can offer, not what we can give to them. But we really don't need to get filled up in order to give: Giving fills us up. The secret to enriching relationships is to give more of ourselves.

~~~~~~~

> But we really don't need to get filled up in
> order to give: Giving fills us up.

~~~~~~~

I heard a story about a young man who struggled financially while his older brother was a huge success in the theatre. For Christmas, the elder brother decided to share his good fortune with his family by giving them each the present of their dreams. Although this younger brother could barely make payments on his run-down hatchback, he yearned for a sports car. And that's what he received. So thrilled was he with this fabulous gift, he drove and drove in no particular direction and wound up in an impoverished neighborhood. There on a street corner stood a little boy in a thin windbreaker staring awestruck at the gorgeous car. The young man revved the engine a few times for show, then rolled down his window so his young admirer could get a peek at the leather interior. He said, "Hey, kid, how you doin'?"

The kid said, "Wow, that's a really cool car."

"Yep. My brother gave it to me for Christmas."

And the little boy said, "Man, someday I hope . . ." and the young man was thinking the kid would finish, ". . . I have a brother like that."

But what the child said instead was, "Man, someday I hope I'm a brother like that."

Are we a brother like that? A sister? Parent? Partner? Friend? Or do we sometimes treat love the way many people do money, hoarding what we have for fear of not getting enough? We can be spiritually generous or stay trapped in poverty thinking. When our soul feels impoverished, we cling to any idea, money or love that comes our way, reluctant to share, because we might lose what little we have. We begrudge others their abundance, unless they give back in kind. We don't give freely, for worry over what it's going to cost us. We penny-pinch compliments, as if acknowledging another person's success steals our own chances. Do we better ourselves by hoarding? Of course not; eventually, we will declare spiritual bankruptcy, because our inner life is empty.

But if we are spiritually generous, our relationship account never runs out. Imagine living in a state of absolute spiritual well-being. You awaken each morning anticipating the day's gifts. You are filled to overflowing with the bounty of life and can hardly wait to see how you will share the greatness of this day with others. Does this sound too good to be true, Pollyanna-like, perhaps? Well, what I know through experience is that anyone who develops a close, conscious contact with his or her Creator grows relationships just this way.

If we are spiritually generous,
our relationship account never runs out.

When Mother Teresa first told her superiors in Rome that God had given her a dream to build a mission in India, she was asked: "How much money do you have?"

She answered: "I have three pennies."

Everyone laughed at her. She was told: "With three pennies you cannot build anything."

The tiny nun, all four foot eight inches of her, stood up and replied: "With three pennies and God, I can build anything."

Mother Teresa went on to build 517 orphanages, homes for the poor, AIDS hospices and charity centers in a hundred countries throughout the world.

With three pennies and God, you can build any relationships you desire, because those who are spiritually generous will never want for anything. Giving doesn't empty your soul; rather, it literally expands the giver.

At our deepest level, most of us really do want to be generous with our minds, hearts and pocketbooks. Somewhere along the way, however, we start attaching requirements to giving. We tally who gave what last. We withhold our love until the other person gives his or her share. And relationships that might have flourished wither after the first bloom.

Generosity operates at three levels. At the first level, giving demands compensation, because we *Give to Get*. We nickel-and-dime emotions, never giving an iota of comfort or support for free. There's got to be something in it for us; we're like people who donate monetarily in order to receive accolades for their "generosity."

Jesus spoke sharply about such givers. He said: "Take heed that you do not do your charitable deeds before men, to be seen by them. Otherwise you have no reward from your Father in heaven. Therefore when you do a charitable deed, do not sound a trumpet before you as the hypocrites do . . . that they may have glory from men."

Those who are truly generous require no accolade, finding instead a greater gift of connection with God. We have a generous God who provides everything we need and more, but so many of us operate as orphans, with thoughts of scarcity, that we must get "ours" and hang on.

~~~~~~

Those who are truly generous require no accolade,
finding instead a greater gift of connection with God.

~~~~~~

You may have heard that good relationships are 50-50, each person giving an equal share. Perhaps, but *great* relationships require 100-100. Otherwise, we fall into a quid pro quo mentality, thinking all the time that we never want to give more than the other person. Sometimes, one partner cannot give his or her share, and correspondingly, our own energy drops. You can't stand outside a woodstove and say, "You give me heat, then I'll give you wood." Nobody warms up that way. And no relationship can thrive when every act of giving is predicated on how much the other gave first. The 50-50 equation demands *Give to Get:* I'll be kind to you, so long as you are equally good to me.

Giving to get doesn't fulfill us. We feel tense or begrudging, anticipating a reward and believing ourselves cheated if that reward is not forthcoming. In fact, we are cheating ourselves out of the joy that giving freely brings. If we give by percentages, we'll start to measure who's doing more. We'll want to hold back when our partner or child appears to give less.

I'm not suggesting that we become martyrs or give unendingly to unhealthy relationships, only that we recognize and touch our inherent generosity. God, whose generosity is without bounds, doesn't keep score. And neither should we. With an altruistic approach to the heart, we share freely our ideas, our affections and ourselves and look for the positive intention in one another. We are not meant to hoard love, but to share it through philanthropy of the soul, the practice of spiritual generosity.

The second level of generosity is *Give with Strings*. At this level, we do not so much seek equal measure, but are very selective and may become judgmental about who deserves our attention, caring or compassion.

There's an old expression about giving with one hand and taking away with the other. After Jesus laments the temple-goers who make a show out of giving, he suggests: ". . . when you do a charitable deed, do not let your left hand know what your right hand is doing that your charitable deed may be in secret and your Father who sees in secret will . . . reward you openly." This means we do not allow judgment to constrict our generosity. If one hand (part of us) wants to give, another part may recoil, for fear of giving too much. If you give freely, your "father," that divine, generous presence within, responds. You begin to align your behavior with your being.

This philosophy applies equally to relationships. By casting judgment, we shortchange our generosity.

My friend Carolyn discovered this after she looked outside her window one day to see a large motor home parked almost in front of her house. The streets in her neighborhood are extremely narrow, so this motorized behemoth with California plates proved quite an obstacle every time Carolyn pulled into or out of her driveway.

Yet Carolyn accepted the inconvenience gracefully. After all, her neighbors were a sweet, elderly couple. "They've been so good to me over the years," she thought. "I bet their kids have come from California for a visit."

So every time Carolyn backed out of the driveway, craning her neck to watch for oncoming cars, she said to herself, "Well, I'm glad their kids are here to see them," and off she went.

On the fifth day, she learned that the motor home belonged not to the children of the sweet elderly couple next door, but to friends of the ornery couple across the street. These neighbors left their trash bins out all week long, complained incessantly whenever a dog dared bark and never had a kind word for anyone.

Immediately, the motor home became a monster. "Every time I had to back out of the driveway, every time I came home, this tense, angry feeling rose in my gut," she says. "I thought, 'Isn't it just like them to inconvenience the whole neighborhood with this eyesore, and not even care.' "

The motor home had been parked in the same place all along. What had moved was not the vehicle, but her perception. When she thought the motor home belonged to the children of a sweet old couple, she accepted the inconvenience without judgment. She wanted good for others—if she liked them. But how could the neighborhood pain-in-the-necks enjoy themselves at her inconvenience!

There's an old proverb: "Your own soul is nourished when you are kind, and destroyed when you are cruel." When we offer kindness, giving even to those we think unworthy, we are in alignment with our true nature. We inherit this nature from God, the essence of spiritual generosity. We are in integrity with our true nature when we give loving kindness. And it feels so good!

Kahlil Gibran wrote in *The Prophet:* "You say, I would give, but only to the deserving. The trees in your orchard say not so. They give that they shall live, for to withhold is to perish."

Give to Live is the highest level of generosity. My son Mat has a friend named Jason whom he's known since second grade. Both natural athletes, they competed against one another in every sport from kickball to hockey until sixth grade, when they discovered football. Soon another player—Craig—came along whose grace on the field rivaled their own, and those three boys decided that instead of trying to vie against one another for the top post, they would pool their individual strengths and help one another become the best football players in the school. The threesome was inseparable. Every afternoon those boys would scrimmage and run plays and hoot and holler whenever one of them made a touchdown.

Two years later, Craig was diagnosed with a malignant brain tumor. He underwent radiation and chemotherapy, which made him lose his hair and impaired his motor skills—permanently. Craig could no longer keep up; his movements were stiff and awkward. In high school, Jason was the team's quarterback, Mat the star running back. Craig volunteered to be the team's water boy.

Senior year, Jason and Mat were once again competing, this time for King of the May Fete. The boys nominated to the court had to give a speech to the entire school. The topic was heroes. The high school auditorium was packed full of eighteen hundred rowdy teenagers, as one by one the would-be kings spoke about their heroes, their words punctuated by cheers and shouting. One boy talked about Abraham Lincoln, another about Jesus, and another said his hero was Albert Einstein. Mat gave a great talk, and I was very proud.

Then Jason got up. He very much wanted to be crowned king. As he'd told us earlier, being king was cool. You attracted the girls, not to mention the fact that the title looked impressive on your college application.

But there was something he wanted more than the votes of his classmates. He wanted to honor his real hero.

"My hero is someone you all know," he began. "His name is Craig."

This was a risky thing to do, because Craig had been made the brunt of a number of jokes by people who didn't understand his illness. The teenagers who'd ridiculed him were sitting in the auditorium.

"He's my hero," Jason went on, "because I've seen him display awesome courage in the face of overwhelming adversity. I saw him be really afraid and face his fear when he thought he might die. I've seen him remain strong in the face of cruel comments and put-downs. He's my hero because he is so strong. He didn't like what happened to his body, but he accepts it. Craig always wanted to be part of the football team, and I think he is the *heart* of our team. My hope is that someday I might live up to the example of my hero, Craig."

The auditorium was silent. Jason knew he had sacrificed his opportunity to be crowned king. But he didn't care.

Then a lone clap sounded from the back of the auditorium. Soon it spread to a thunderous applause, the student body rising to its feet. As I sat in the auditorium that day, rooting for my own son to be named king, tears of gratitude rolled down my face for the tremendous generosity Jason had displayed. In less than a minute, he had taken the minds of eighteen hundred students and shifted them. He spoke out for his hero and friend, and he spoke out for every other "Craig" any of these kids might encounter throughout their lives. Jason was named King of the May Fete. But the honor extended well beyond a crown.

Jesus said, "A city that is set on a hill cannot be hidden. Nor do they light a lamp and put it under a basket, but on a lamp stand, and it gives light to all who are in the house. Let your light so shine before others that they may see your good works and glorify God." Let your light so shine.

It was one thing for Jason to admire Craig privately. But when he took the risk to let his generosity shine, everyone in that auditorium caught some of the light. Jason received the gift of wanting to be a better person because of someone else. And he became one. He became *a brother like that*. Love is the thought that brings light to any situation.

〰〰〰〰

Love is the thought that brings light to any situation.

〰〰〰〰

THOUGHTS THAT TRANSFORM

To enrich my relationships I can begin to:

~ Give without keeping score.

~ Give when I don't appear to be getting anything back.

~ Give attention.

~ Give compassion.

~ Give the benefit of the doubt.

~ Give to live.

PRACTICE

Ask yourself, "What has been one of my most difficult acts of generosity?" For me, the answer's easy. My husband and I were taking an anniversary vacation in Arizona and having lunch at a lovely historical inn. Ed was wearing a string of beads on his arm that our waitress admired greatly. The year before, the Dalai Lama himself had blessed those beads during a visit I had with him. To be able to present such a gift to my husband meant more to me than I can say. The entire plane ride home, I kept imagining his face when he unwrapped this sacred, precious gift that could be bought in no store the world over. The waitress was even more enthralled after hearing the story of their origin.

"You really seem to like them," Ed told her, pulling the strand off his wrist. "Why don't you just keep them."

The waitress was speechless, and so was I. Sputtering is not my normal mode of speech, but I could barely contain myself.

After the waitress left our table, I said, "How could you . . . ? Those beads are my gift . . . I gave you those . . . That's not what I *wanted . . ." And so forth.*

Ed replied, "I just felt that she should have them, in that moment."

"How dare he ruin my gift that way?" I thought. But somewhere inside, spiritual practice arose, and I heard the words from A Course in Miracles: *"I must have chosen wrongly, because I am not at peace."*

I was not at peace. I believed my gift to Ed to be one of unstinting generosity, but the truth is, I wanted Ed to cherish those beads the way I wanted him to cherish them: by wearing them around his arm. His giving them away meant he didn't value me.

Many people would agree with me that what Ed did was not reasonable. And they'd be right. Ed was demonstrating unreasonable giving, which is giving for the pure joy of making another person happy. Ed's proclivity for unreasonable giving is one of the reasons I love him. He has impulses toward generosity and follows them. He gives to live.

Our waitress returned to our table, glowing with happiness. "You know, the farthest I've ever gone in my life, and I'm twenty-two years old, is Phoenix. That's a hundred and ten miles away, but I have dreams of traveling. Just to have some-thing this amazing from a world away is a symbol. It gives me hope that I really am going to go somewhere. I really am."

Ouch.

I felt about two inches tall. But that episode gave me a gift I'll never forget. I received the gift of seeing that although I considered myself a generous person, I gave with strings attached. I wanted Ed's gratitude, and the strings on my gift were that he would use them the way I deemed best.

It's when we find ourselves looking square in the face of our shortcomings that we find the opportunity to grow in love. None of us are perfect. We're not asking to be perfect. But we can stretch from where we are now. We can strive for a "personal best." It's only when we come up against a record that we set before that we're able to love in a greater way than we did yesterday.

I mistakenly believed that Ed's giving detracted from what I gave him. The truth is, his act amplified the gift. Every time we talk about that waitress, we both feel wonderful, imagining her planning a trip to some distant land. Spiritual generosity is an ever-upward spiral. So take a closer look at your difficult act of giving. Find the gift you received in return.

11. CREATING SPACE FOR GRACE

Some of the most beautiful meals I've ever enjoyed were lunches served to me in Dharamsala, India, at the Norbulingka Institute, which is home of the Tibetan government in exile. It wasn't the food—spicy Tibetan cuisine doesn't always agree with my digestion—and it certainly wasn't the dishes: chipped china mixed with plastic plates, wooden bowls and cutlery nicked and bent with age. What made these meals memorable was an accompaniment more gracious than anything Martha Stewart could whip up.

I was with a group of fifty religious and political leaders from around the world who were meeting with His Holiness the Dalai Lama to brainstorm ideas on working together for a better world. (It was during this visit that the Dalai Lama blessed the beads.) Unaccustomed to feeding such a large group, the staff stayed up all night to cook the food. At lunchtime, we would form a line, cafeteria style, in front of the buffet. There, at the head of the line, stood a server next to a stack of plates. As each person approached the buffet, the server would pick up a plate, gaze down into it and pour out a blessing for the person about to eat. Bowing, the server would then gently place the plate in the guest's hands.

What a generous act of love, that someone would take the effort to honor guests in such a fashion! Eating off Limoges would not have felt half as special. I couldn't help but think of some of the dinners I've slapped down in front of my family, saying nothing more profound than, "Here, better eat it before it gets cold."

Like the Tibetan waiters, we can turn everyday activities into acts of gracious generosity. We don't have to spend a fortune in order to make giving a way of life. How we serve a meal, address our children, greet our coworkers or conduct business can all reflect gratitude and generosity. It just takes a slight shift in perspective. You know the expression "taking for granted"? Sometimes we make assumptions about what's due us and then neglect to feel grateful. We can take for granted anything from food on the table to the presence of loved ones. "Taking for granted" means that we assume what someone else does for us is our due. It's all about taking. What if instead we were "giving for granted"? We would automatically assume it is our responsibility to enrich the lives of others. We can give to any relationship by making an everyday activity special, so that even something as ordinary as serving a meal can become an extraordinary experience.

The shift from taking to giving starts through praise and acknowledgment. People feel loved when they are acknowledged. The word "acknowledgment" contains the words "know" and "gem." Ask yourself: Do I know the gem in everyone I meet? On a daily basis, am I looking for people to praise? Or do I primarily focus on getting things done? We don't have to look far to find good. Acknowledge your child for starting his homework without being told, your spouse for making the coffee each morning, the grocery carrier who stands patiently in the pouring rain with your sacks while you fumble for your car keys.

We can extend this same spirit of giving beyond our immediate circle. During my visit with the Dalai Lama, he taught a spiritual practice that has greatly influenced my relationships.

It's called *compassionate breathing*, and I now practice it every morning. His Holiness explained the philosophy behind compassionate breathing: "You must begin by cherishing yourself. All religions teach that you must love yourself first. It is essential to the progress of the world. To cherish oneself is not easy. We are all sacred beings, but we do not see each other or ourselves as such. We must train ourselves. We must cherish the life we are given and cherish the life of others."

There are four parts to the Dalai Lama's practice:

First, remember, no matter how differently you see yourself from others, we all want the same thing: to avoid suffering and find happiness.

Second, remembering this universal commonality, begin each day with five minutes of compassionate breathing. Take air in, cherishing yourself. The practice allows you to cultivate the same feeling for yourself as you have for a treasured loved one. As you breathe in, imagine a loved one, noticing your feelings of appreciation, compassion and protectiveness. Then substitute that person's image with your own, building that same kind of unconditional love for yourself. Even if your heart is in pain, recognize that God has given you life and exercise your appreciation for this gift. Then breathe out, cherishing others. Think kindly upon those you know; wish the best for humankind in its entirety. Cherishing yourself as you breathe in, cherishing others breathing out, you begin to build an awareness of the spiritual connectedness of all life. With kindness as your foundation, you begin to see others more compassionately.

Third, extend that compassion throughout the day. Forgive someone close to you. Practice thinking kindly of those who have wronged you, wishing only for their well-being.

Finally, remain faithful to the practice. Even if you don't see results right away, never forget that we all desire happiness. Put that belief into action by helping others find their own happiness.

Scripture instructs us: "Be doers of the Word, not hearers only." If I hear the words of the Dalai Lama, I'm inspired. I say to myself, "Yes, those are good teachings," but if I don't really embody or apply them, nothing more than inspiration has occurred. Nothing will have changed. Inspiration is nice, but not until we take action do we move into transformation.

Sometimes, when we feel overwhelmed—by strained relationships, or even by the violence that seems to have crept into every crevice of society—there's a tendency to think: "What can I do? What difference can one person make?" It's easy to think that the world will improve through somebody else's effort, somebody with more to give than us. The truth is, nobody has more to give than you. Martin Luther King didn't sit back and say, "Somebody ought to fight for civil rights." Gandhi didn't say, "How could one Indian attorney transform a nation?" These individuals recognized and applied their authority as children of God through action. There is a power in you that can change your world. This force may not have caught fire with anyone else you know, but if you pay attention, you will find it burning in you, right at this moment.

~~~~~~

> There is a power in you that can change your world.
> This force may not have caught fire with anyone else
> you know, but if you pay attention, you will find it
> burning in you, right at this moment.

~~~~~~

"Do" means action. Regardless of how we feel, we can reach out and help somebody else. When I'm feeling at my lowest, what I need to do most is offer an encouraging word. There is a child who needs a book read to him or her, an elderly neighbor who needs company. In the act of making something else better, I better myself. Remember, we are wired up to feel good when we do good. Taking generous action guides us to grace. In that state of grace, we begin to see, in a myriad of ways, how life blesses us.

Think about what you can *do*. A real estate investor who attends our church told me that even as his material success grew, he felt something missing in his life. Dick considered himself a generous person and was the first to share his wealth with those less fortunate. Yet just giving money didn't feel like enough.

Dick has dyslexia and recalls the pain he felt as a child struggling with schoolwork. Letters and words seemed to reverse themselves at random, and just when he thought he had mastered a new word, it would crop up again on the same page, appearing as if for the first time. The other kids ridiculed him and his teachers thought him lazy, at best. Dick never forgot how it felt to be labeled stupid, and came to realize that a major contribution he could make was in giving to children with disabilities. He began taking off a half-day a week to volunteer in a special education classroom at an elementary school.

Dick counts among the greatest moments in his life the time he asked a little boy, "Jimmy, I've seen you make such progress these past two years—what do you think has made the difference?" and the little boy responded, "I've had you here to believe in me."

~~~~~~~~

"Imagine if everybody asked themselves, 'What can I *do*?' and then went and actually did something."

~~~~~~~~

A woman in our congregation turned inspiration to transformation following the tragedy at Columbine High School. Her teenage children were frightened, particularly because the shooting didn't happen in a crime-ridden, violent setting, but at a quiet, suburban high school much like their own.

Her children started noticing outcasts, kids who were ridiculed and friendless. Maybe, they worried, their school would become the next Columbine. "We're scared, Mom," they said.

Karen wanted to comfort her children, but the issue felt too big for her. "What can *I* do?" she thought. "This is a national problem, not something a mom can do much about." Then her thinking shifted to "What can I *do?*" and an idea struck her that seemed so simple: Why not see to it that no one got left out? Karen, with her children's help, formed a group of teenagers who agreed to reach out to friendless students. The kids would say hello to them in the hallways, join them for lunch in the cafeteria and include them in school activities. Once a week, the students got together to come up with ideas to induce others to participate in what Karen called the Acts of Kindness team. The idea caught fire, and soon Karen was helping to establish Acts of Kindness teams at other high schools. Students began wearing buttons that read: "Kindness Happens." And when some of those students took a school trip to Washington, D.C., they wore their buttons, which generated questions from local youngsters, who began the same kind of team in their own schools.

Karen said she never dreamed that an ordinary mom could make such a difference. "Imagine if everybody asked themselves, 'What can I *do?*' and then went and actually did something." Karen said what surprised her even more is how her own life has been altered. "I feel so wonderful about making a difference, it's changed all my relationships," she said.

There is one more step that will complete your shift from taking to giving, and that is to *give love anonymously:* Do not limit your giving solely to those who can acknowledge your generosity. At least once a day, perform a loving act for someone else without taking any credit. Mow your elderly neighbor's yard when she's away from home. Pick up litter in the parking lot. Feed a stray animal. Buy cookies for the senior center. If you normally run the PTA or give speeches on behalf of the homeless, you already get brownie points. People may notice your giving, and that is wonderful. But there is another gift that comes when we learn to give without anyone knowing about it. Volunteer at the warehouse where people are packing crates of food to send to the needy overseas or across the country. Let no one learn of your good deeds.

At first, this may drive your ego nuts; it wants to be rewarded for giving. You ego wants to say, "Look what I'm doing. Look how good I am." But remember: Anytime we remove our ego from a situation, we create a space for grace to flow into us and through all our relationships.

There's a man at our church who routinely orders pizza for the entire staff, and the employees have no idea who is the source of their lunchtime treat. At our cafeteria, he'll give the cashier money for the next ten people in line, on the condition she keep his identity secret. And he walks away, never seeing the faces of the people who enjoy his generosity.

This man says that he gives so that others can feel that life *is* generous. "If people can't attach a gift to any one person, they attach it to everybody," he says. "They become nice to more than one person." It enhances their attitude, he says, creating a chain of generosity and goodwill.

Our anonymous congregant says he inevitably winds up feeling better himself. Often, he's feeling trapped by a "brain freeze" in a business decision and gets a nudge to give. "And every time, my own attitude shifts, which enables me to be less preoccupied with my own problems. I suddenly refocus, and the things I thought were overwhelming are no longer so big. Work becomes less strenuous, so I go home and am able to focus on what's really important, and that's my relationship with God and with my family."

~~~~~~

THOUGHTS THAT TRANSFORM

~ To increase my loving, I focus on what I can contribute to others, instead of what others should be giving to me.

~ I remember, "Nothing is more powerful than love in action."

~ I shift from "taking for granted" to "giving for granted" by looking for others to acknowledge on a daily basis.

PRACTICE

Ask yourself, "What can I do?"

There have been some special people who have made a real difference in your life. Maybe your fifth-grade math teacher revealed in you a real talent for figures. Maybe an old friend gave you a compliment when it was needed. I think it is part of God's plan for us that we encounter these life-giving people who, for some mystical reason, assist us to come alive in their presence and give us just what we most need. Compile a list of people who have contributed to you in some way. Consider them your benefactors. Close your eyes and hold gratitude for them in your heart, sending each a silent blessing.

Go a step further and let them know the difference they have made. Drop one or two of them a note letting them know how their generosity impacted your life. Imagine how you would feel to open your mail and receive a card from someone you assisted five, ten or even twenty years ago! I know a man named Brian who, as a teenager, was greatly influenced by a family friend who shared with Brian his love of travel. Hearing of the older man's adventures whetted the boy's appetite to see the world, and he wound up traveling the globe several times over. Decades later, when the family friend was too old and frail to travel on his own, Brian hired an escort and sent him on a final trip to Europe. The older man had a wonderful time, but the person who most delighted in the experience was Brian, who'd traveled an even greater distance. He'd journeyed from head to heart by finding just the right way to express his gratitude.

Compile a gratitude list. Write down ten things for which you're grateful. When the day is done, read your list. And sometime tomorrow, add five more things, reading your list nightly. The next day, add four more, and that evening, read your expanded list. Keep adding until you reach a number that causes you to stretch to come up with new gratitudes. For the next month, add at least one gratitude a day. If you are willing to do this simple exercise with an open heart and mind, willing to feel the gratitude each item on your list represents, you'll notice a big change in your life very shortly. You're going to start paying attention to wondrous blessings: The fresh smell of coffee. The gentle touch of your child's hand. The friend who called unexpectedly just to say hello. And as you start paying attention with gratitude, you'll notice that your whole inner life is amplified, that your sense of worth has blossomed. After all, only a worthy person could have been given so many blessings. Instead of "taking for granted," you will feel so blessed that you begin giving spontaneously—"giving for granted."

12. You Matter to Me

During a televised interview, a reporter once asked Mother Teresa about her relationship with God. "So, when you're praying, what do you say?"

She replied, "I don't say anything to God. I listen."

"And what does God say to you?"

Mother Teresa answered: "He doesn't say anything to me. He listens."

Words were superfluous in the silent communion between Mother Teresa and God. Theirs was such a close, powerful connection that the human need to explain, justify or beseech fell away. Why use language to express what the heart and mind already communicate more purely? God was listening to her deepest thoughts without her expressing them; she was *being* as one with her Creator. Mother Teresa didn't need to set time aside to listen to God, because she was never not listening.

Can we, as ordinary mortals, ever achieve this level of communion? Some of the sweetest moments of any relationship occur in wordless connection. The lines between you and me cease to exist, separation fades away and two beings become as one. Most people only find that level of oneness during the sexual act. In making love, the individual blurs as a beautiful dance of togetherness emerges. But it is possible to experience the mystery of one another's presence beyond the physical act.

～～～～～

Some of the sweetest moments of any relationship occur in wordless connection.

～～～～～

In the midst of an openhearted relationship, there can be a sense of oneness without touch. Parents can sit across the room from one another, or even be in different cities, and still feel that communion with their child. Friends who haven't seen one another in years need only think of the other person to feel supported. Words are unnecessary. But listening is mandatory. We move toward a sense of oneness in our relationships by practicing authentic listening.

In the biblical Book of James, we read, "Let everyone be quick to listen, slow to speak and slow to anger." Many times, in an effort to be helpful, I have spoken too quickly, saying something that was harsh or insensitive, self-promoting or just plain foolish. Later, I've chastised myself: "Why did I talk so much?"

Never have I chastised myself, "Why did I listen so much?" When we interrupt or merely wait for our opportunity to speak, we may be conversing but not really listening. Our agendas remain separate. The other person seeks to be heard. We want to be heard *more*. Listening then becomes nothing more than our chance to plan a witty retort.

～～～～～

Think of listening as a gift you give someone else.

～～～～～

Try to think of listening as a gift you give someone else. We give our full attention. If we can listen without judging or offering advice, our entire focus shifts outside ourselves. There are no strings attached. With the shared purpose of understanding, two people act as one.

Many years ago, I read about a study in which people from different walks of life were asked: "What is the most profound way you feel loved?" The number one response was "When someone is really listening." By devoting our full attention to another, what we really offer is love. Genuine listening is saying in a language more powerful than words: *You matter to me.*

Ask yourself: Am I a giving listener? Listening is akin to driving in that we tend to rate ourselves as more proficient than others might. The person you absentmindedly cut off on the freeway while thinking about that upcoming meeting might have some choice comments on your driving. Your children, spouse and best friend probably have a thing or two to say about a time they couldn't get your attention. I've never asked anyone to critique my driving (the police have offered their opinion un-solicited), but I have asked my son to rate my listening.

In my line of work, the ability to listen well is a kind of pre-requisite for the job. Maybe I was looking for kudos, but when I asked Mat, "How well do you think I listen to you?" the answer surprised me.

"Sometimes you listen just great," he said, "like I feel that everything I say really matters. But other times," he added, "other times you just *act* like you're listening. And I feel like that whatever you're really thinking about is more important than me."

My relationship with my son is precious, yet when I don't truly devote energy to hearing what he has to say, how can he help but feel diminished? Sometimes we pretend to listen, waiting for pauses so that we can fill them with an appropriate "Oh, really?" or "That's nice," rather than taking the time to be honest. Mat said he'd prefer me to postpone a conversation than to only half-listen. That made sense to me. As much as I love my children, I can't always drop whatever I'm doing to hear them out. It's fine to say, "I really want to be able to listen to you, but now isn't a good time. What about in an hour? Or later tonight?"

Consider the following practices to build your skills as a giving listener.

Ask two or three loved ones to rate your listening skills. Solicit suggestions. Mat and I worked out a cue system for when I drift into half-listening. When he senses my attention waning, he simply lets me know by saying, "Hello?" and I either focus in or we set a time to talk later. As a result, our relationship has grown closer during his late teens and early twenties, a time when so many parents lose touch with their young adult children. Relationships that satisfy both parties don't happen by accident; we create them.

Another way to listen more is to *talk less.* Take a breath. Practice not interrupting by listening not only to the words but to the silence that follows. Have you ever wondered if you talk too much? Think for a moment. When you speak, do you ever see people's eyes wander? Do you ever have to follow their gaze and mentally pull them back in?

Having attended lectures and conferences on several continents, I've been privileged to hear many world-class speakers. Often, their words have had a profound impact on me, but none so much as the world-class listeners, especially His Holiness, the Dalai Lama. What struck me immediately about him was the intensity with which he listened. For him, listening is anything but a passive exercise. It is spiritual practice. With his left palm opened upward, as if in meditation, and his gaze fixed steadily upon whomever was speaking, his entire being was devoted to understanding the other person. Even in a crowded room, the person talking felt as if he or she was the only person in the universe at that moment, and that the universe was a loving one. No one ever felt hurried. The Dalai Lama communicated volumes with his gaze, encouraging the speaker to express thoughts and feelings freely. He treated each speaker with the same reverence as if God were speaking, and in doing so, saw the God in each person who spoke.

When we talk less, we listen more. Through authentically listening, we can send the message: *What matters to you matters to me.* One afternoon, when my son Rich was about five years old, his friends came to the front door to play, but he had vanished. They stood there, literally twiddling their thumbs, while I searched the house, finally locating him in the laundry room. He was sitting in front of the clothes dryer.

"Rich," I said, "your friends are waiting for you. What are you doing here?"

"I'm waiting for my socks to dry."

"You've got plenty of socks," I told him. "Grab another pair."

"No," he insisted. "I want the blue ones that match my pants."

"Get another pair and go join your friends. It doesn't matter what socks you wear."

This little blond boy stood up, put his hands on his hips and announced, "Well, it matters to me."

The vision of that barefooted child sitting poised in front of the dryer, waiting for his socks to dry, has stayed with me all these years, because I learned something about listening that day. If I loved my son, then what mattered to him mattered to me. It wasn't my job to make what mattered to me matter to him.

When we talk less, we listen more.

As we practice the skills that make us giving listeners for others, we ourselves hear more deeply. We tune in more deeply to God. Paying attention in the moment is an ancient practice that makes us feel more peaceful and centered. Gandhi once said, "For me, the Voice was more real than my own existence. It has never failed me, or for that matter, anyone else. And everyone who wills can hear the Voice. It is within everyone. But like everything else, it requires previous and definite preparation." No words are necessary.

~~~~~~

THOUGHTS THAT TRANSFORM

God has designed my body in accordance with how I am meant to live:

~ My ears are higher than my mouth, meaning that I should listen before I speak.

~ My ears open to the front and sides, meaning that I should listen to those before me and beside me rather than tuning in to what is said behind my back.

~ My cochlea, or inner ear, is not visible to the eye, but without it, sound would have no meaning. I am meant to listen not just outwardly, but to the inner voice that is my voice for God.

PRACTICE

~During a calm, peaceful moment, ask a loved one to rate your listening skills. (After an argument, you're likely to get a biased answer.) Ask that person for examples of when he or she has felt truly loved, and times that you've fallen short. Ask for suggestions to improve your skills.

Here are a few suggestions that all of us can utilize to become more giving listeners:

~*MAKE EYE CONTACT. We are told that Jesus had the ability to see everyone truly. He looked beyond history or appearance and saw the true being, offering an opportunity for healing. We can offer the same gift. Listen to more than the words; hear the tone, watch expressions and peer into the soul. In so doing, we offer another the opportunity to feel loved. It doesn't matter if the speaker is our partner or the stranger sitting next to us on the bus. Eye contact nourishes the speaker with your loving attention.*

~*PAY ATTENTION. Sounds simple, but we tend to pay attention to what we're thinking instead of the other person. We've got our comeback planned before he or she has finished speaking. The message sent is that what I think or feel is more important than what you think and feel. So let's forget about how witty we'll sound in response. Instead, absorb everything that's said without jumping ahead. The simple act of listening feeds your relationship. This is a relationship that you value, and your attention builds an emotional bank account that will pay dividends in your closeness.*

~*Select one point you'd like to know more about and say, "TELL ME MORE." Maybe you think you already understand everything the other person has said. It doesn't matter. Saying "Tell me more" invites the two of you to a deeper level of sharing. You just might surprise yourself. Ask questions with genuine interest.*

~*NEVER BETRAY A CONFIDENCE. Keep what you learn to yourself. As listeners, we hold a sacred trust.*

FLUENT IN THE LANGUAGE OF THE HEART

SPIRITUAL PRINCIPLE
Love is never complete until it is expressed.

To love another person is to see the face of God.

—VICTOR HUGO

13. SLEEPING WITH FROGS

Of all the biblical plagues, perhaps none has had a more lasting impression on me than the frogs. That's because no matter how much we'd like to confine the invasion of those slimy little amphibians to the pages of Exodus, they continue to hop into and muck up our modern-day relationships.

The story of Exodus recounts the deliverance of the Israelites from Egyptian bondage after 430 years. Moses demands, "Let my people go!" which doesn't much impress Pharaoh, given that the Israelites have been enslaved for centuries. Why should he listen to this upstart? Moses, however, is on a "mission from God." When Pharaoh refuses, God sends in the frogs.

Visualize millions of frogs crawling up your dining table, covering the food, hopping across your body. Imagine tossing and turning all night, unable to block out the chorus of ribbeting on your bed. Think about breaking open a loaf of bread to find a bulging-eyed baked green body inside. Pharaoh, repulsed and highly agitated, sends for Moses, promising he'll let the Israelites go free—just get rid of those frogs!

"When?" Moses asks, to which Pharaoh replies: "Tomorrow."

Tomorrow? "What can this man be thinking?" Moses wondered. At his word, the blight that was making life intolerable could be removed in an instant, but he decides, "I'm going to spend another night in absolute, unrelenting misery."

Pharaoh not only put up with those slimy creatures for an-other night, he went back on his word. "He hardened his heart," leaving the Israelites enslaved. Did Pharaoh really think he could outwit God? God, being infinite, wasn't about to run short of pestilence. Sure enough, the plagues just kept coming. Lice in-fested the land, along with flies and locusts, and the Egyptian population broke out in hideous boils.

But Pharaoh was not unique in his decision to sleep with frogs. We know what we deeply desire: We want love. We want intimacy. We want rich, rewarding relationships that leave us vibrantly, electrifyingly alive. We want our children to confide in us, our parents to enjoy us, our friends to trust us, neighbors and coworkers to feel fortunate we're in their lives. And vice versa.

Still, at times, we just can't resist cozying up with the am-phibians.

I have found that we have a divine side in us that knows what we must do. I also know that we have a very human nature that is less confident. The human part longs for intimacy but doesn't al-ways trust the risks we must take to achieve love. We don't want to give up the known for the unknown, even if the status quo is not fulfilling. When *we* sleep with frogs, it doesn't pose a na-tional health hazard or cast a scourge upon the landscape. But it surely does sap our relationships. We might feel an inner nudge: "Tell this person how you truly feel"; but we respond, "Sure, let me get back to you on that." Though we recognize that we need to set aside grudges and resentments and judgments of others, we say, "But I'm just not ready. Tomorrow, I'll deal with it. Tomorrow."

~~~~~~

I have found that we have a divine side in us that
knows what we must do. I also know that we have a
very human nature that is less confident.

~~~~~~

Pharaoh knew what to do: Let the Israelites leave Egypt! But wanting to retain control at any cost, he must have reasoned, "Well, I want those frogs gone, but not if I have to give up my labor force."

We recognize that turning a cold shoulder to a difficult coworker or employer brings stress. We know that yelling at our children every time they misbehave only alienates them. We know that letting the kids eat dinner in front of the television prevents communication and sharing. We know precisely what depletes our relationships, but we choose to tolerate the intolerable for one more day. Have you ever gone into debt, then filled out an application for a new credit card? Have you ever postponed making a difficult phone call? Every day it gets harder, until finally, we don't dial at all. But we toss and turn all night, because we've chosen to sleep one more night with the frogs.

We say: "I want to be debt-free, but I really don't want to give up that high when I buy something"; "I really want intimacy. I want this relationship to work, but I don't want to give up feeling righteous. Let's make that other person suffer just a little longer"; "I want to meet someone special, but I don't want to give up feeling sorry for myself"; "I want my relationships to work, but I don't want to give up putting others down, because it makes me feel better right then."

So we spend another night with the frogs. We long for intimacy but make choices that keep us distanced. Fortunately, we have the capacity to choose a better way. "Exodus" literally means "the way out." We can free ourselves from bondage whenever we choose. We have all got a Moses side, a side that works through Higher Power. As a minister I know puts it: "Moses tells us, 'God gave me a can of Frog-Be-Gone. Just tell me when. I'll exercise this power anytime you tell me.' "

I nearly forgot my Frog-Be-Gone during a casual party at our house for my stepson. We invited Michael's mother and her family over before Michael went off to college. Ed, who's a big cartoon fan, was wearing a Tweety Bird sweatshirt. Prior to the party, I had greeted him with a big hug and said, "Hi there, Tweety!"

During the party, just as Ed left to pick up Chinese food, his former wife called out, "Bye, Tweety!"

I knew it didn't mean anything. I knew it was an innocent comment on her part. I knew that what I really wanted was for Michael to be part of a large, loving, open family. In my sermons, I've talked about creating a blended family where real love exists, where no one is shut out. Michael's mother and I have learned to coparent the children and respect each other. We are friends who share Christmas gifts. So I could have just laughed along with everyone else, without taking her remark personally.

Instead, my stomach lurched. I felt like lashing out, "Hey, *I* call him Tweety. *You* don't call him Tweety anymore. If you don't know the rules, let *me* tell you!" My "little me" wanted full rein.

This was a Pharaoh moment. Granted, it was only a small Pharaoh moment, but it's how we respond to life's daily challenges that determines our responses when larger relationship issues arise. I knew I could either take that feeling and build a pyramid between us, or I could practice more perfect loving.

In this moment of deciding how to respond, I did not say anything aloud. I turned to my Moses side and called on Higher Power: "God, what would love do here?" And immediately came this thought: "Isn't it wonderful to be reminded that love is eternal? My husband and his former wife have two wonderful kids together. They no longer want to be married to one another, but they still care for one another, and that's good. In fact, that's very good."

I met a woman named Lee who had to grapple with a much larger Pharaoh issue. She'd been sleeping with frogs so long, she'd almost become accustomed to the discomfort—but not quite. Lee had grown up with a very abusive mother and wanted nothing to do with the woman. What mattered most to her was her relationship with her own children. She adored them. She vowed to be a better mother than her own had been. But her kids liked Grandma. They visited her in secret. And when Mom found out, she erupted: "How dare you betray me this way? You know how awful Grandma is. Do you really think so little of me that you'd just ignore how I feel?"

The outbursts created distance between Lee and her children. And the kids knew that should they ever dare bring up Grandma in conversation, they'd get another earful of resentment. That led to secrecy in the relationship. The kids knew they were forbidden to trespass in certain parts of their mother's life. They could be open with their mother, but only selectively. Worse yet, the children weren't getting a very healthy image of parent-child relationships. They were learning that love has limits, that love should be withheld unless it's expressed a certain way. Naturally, they began to retreat from their mother. They walked on tiptoe around her moods.

~~~~~~~~

We long for intimacy but make choices that keep us distanced. Fortunately, we have the capacity to choose a better way.

~~~~~~~~

So even though the venomous words were spoken about Grandma, the poison seeped out onto the children.

Lee truly craved closeness with her children. She knew her hatred drove a wedge between her and those she loved most, but she couldn't seem to stop herself. After all, she reasoned, this was her mother's fault. If she'd been a better parent, then Lee and her kids would be just fine. Like Pharaoh, Lee was choosing to put up with the misery of frogs rather than give up the slaves—in this case, her hurt—to which she was entitled.

Lee and I spoke for a long time. We talked about what she

wanted most—and that was greater intimacy with her children. Lee's mother couldn't make that a reality, but Lee could. She could stop resenting her mother—not for her mother's sake, but for her own, and for her relationship with her children. Now, I don't know that Lee and her mother will ever get along easily. What matters is that Lee made a decision to free herself from the pain of her past, making herself available to greater intimacy. She saw how her animosity toward her mother had left her feeling bitter, and how her own children were being held captive by that bitterness. At some level, she had always known this was the case. By ridding herself of frogs, she realized, she could free herself for greater loving.

You know what you really desire: to live in love. You want to be able to speak from the heart, to express love freely. But you can't experience real intimacy if you're sleeping with frogs. Don't wait until tomorrow. Make a choice to do what is required to live in love right now.

Thoughts That Transform

~ I know my heart's desire, even if I do not always act upon it.

~ Today, with God's help, I release bitterness, resentment and the need to always control.

~ Today, with God's help, I choose intimacy over distance.

Practice

One technique for ridding your life of frogs is to "set a personal best."

I was speaking in Canada shortly after the 2000 Olympics in Sydney and watched some television interviews with the country's athletes. Despite their having trained as long and hard as the Americans, they came home with relatively few medals. Yet they weren't so much counting gold as celebrating a personal best. They talked of beating an old record they had set, of trying just a little bit harder than they had before.

We don't need to measure ourselves by what somebody else did. We might come out on top or we might come out underneath. What we want to do is look at where we stand right now—where are your frogs?—and go one better. Step into the next realm of what love can be. Let's say you feel an inner nudge to tell a loved one how you feel, but you worry about risking rejection. Your history is to put off saying what needs to be said. The next time you get that nudge, turn to your Higher Power and ask for guidance. Determine to set a personal best. Go one better this time than you did the time before, and slowly, you will find the frogs in your life replaced with love.

14. A Natural Curiosity

One evening when I was on a business trip, I treated myself to dinner at a nice restaurant. I couldn't help but observe the couple at the next table. I didn't mean to eavesdrop, but it quickly became clear that there wasn't much privacy to invade. Their wedding rings spelled marriage, but other than the man calling his wife "honey," I saw little indication of closeness. After putting down their menus, they worked out the details of transporting their son to his soccer game that weekend, then the conversation lagged. No discussion of the day's events, though their well-tailored suits suggested they'd met for dinner after work. They busied themselves by looking around the restaurant and seemed almost grateful when the food arrived. I wondered if they were that hungry or just anxious to fill the void. Other than commenting briefly on the tenderness of the filet, they remained silent. Never once did they touch. The most animated conversation at the table took place when the woman's cell phone rang in her purse. Once the couple had finished eating, two pairs of eyes turned to the waiter, the man asked for the check and husband and wife filed out of the restaurant.

Provided only the merest glimpse of this couple, my conjecture could be wildly off base, but I have seen that same scene replayed many times over the years. The neutral expressions, the distracted gazes and the lack of conversation tell me that this particular man and woman have lost their natural curiosity about one another. Natural curiosity is a God-given ability designed to develop an ever-deepening closeness between two people.

For example, contrast this couple's demeanor with that of two people on the verge of falling in love. Remember the thrill of getting to know someone new, when every moment is a mystery to be unwrapped? The smallest secret revealed is cherished and savored; the most mundane detail of that person's workaday world fascinates. God has presented us with the most exciting, attractive, interesting creature on earth, and we want to know all. We are naturally curious. Then what happens?

At some point, as we grow more comfortable, the mundane really can get that way and our true love's charming eccentricities start to annoy. We stop asking questions, because there is nothing more to know. Or so we think.

~~~~~~~~~

Remember the thrill of getting to know someone new,
when every moment is a mystery to be unwrapped?
The smallest secret revealed is cherished and savored.

~~~~~~~~~

There's a joke about a couple who've been married over fifty years, and one night in bed the wife looks over at her husband and starts to complain. She says, "You know, when we were first married, you'd reach over and hold my hand. It's been years since you've reached over to hold my hand at night."

Despite his arthritis, he thinks, "Well, I could reach over . . ." so he reaches over and takes her hand.

Not satisfied, she says, "When we were first married, you used to snuggle up with me, and we would lie close to each other. You've been on your side of the bed for years."

Even though he's comfortable in his spot, he cuddles up to his wife on the other side of the bed.

Still not happy, she says, "You used to nibble on my ear."

He throws back the covers and hobbles out of bed into the bathroom. "What are you doing?" she asks.

"I'm getting my teeth."

It's easy to hold hands and snuggle and nibble when everything is new and exciting. But for us to continue expressing love when the relationship appears to wane takes extra focus. Something deeper grows in us when we ignite a spark that has grown dim.

Something deeper grows in us when we ignite a spark that has grown dim.

As a counselor and minister, I am not one to say that we should remain forever in a relationship void of nurturing, loving energy. Sometimes, we need to recognize that we love ourselves enough to let someone go who hasn't the desire or capacity to truly offer what we need. But I have seen far too many couples end a relationship when it hit the doldrums or became difficult. Years later, they've mused that had they only tried harder, maybe they could have grown happy with one another. I've also seen parents who mistook ordinary teenage independence as a sign that they were no longer welcome and withdrew from their children's lives. Years later, both parent and child wished they could talk to one another heart to heart, but they no longer knew how. No place is sadder than a heart filled with regret, when we look back and wonder what might have been.

We don't have to look back and wonder. We can rekindle our "natural curiosity" right now.

Natural curiosity isn't about being nosy. It's a way of seeing loved ones as fluid, changing individuals as opposed to merely symbols of our long-established beliefs about "Mom," "Dad," "son," "daughter" and "spouse."

When you get to know someone initially, you're constructing

a moving picture of that individual. You're in a constant state of discovery. The picture changes and grows. But as your attention shifts from getting to know someone to thinking we know him or her, the picture freezes, becoming a snapshot instead. Yet every one of us continues to change and grow every day. When my husband comes home from work, I don't know what he is fearing or thinking or wondering, unless I show him that I want to find out. The man I have dinner with that night is ever so slightly different from the man I awakened to that morning. I want to keep discovering. The first time Ed held my hand, the hairs on the back of my arm stood up. And after all these years, that hasn't changed. My "natural curiosity" has not ebbed one bit, because I nurture it every day. George Bernard Shaw put it best when he said, "The only sane man I know is my tailor, because he measures me anew each time I see him."

Relationships are eternal. Letting them stagnate goes against our true nature, because God imbues us with sufficient curiosity to last a lifetime. Our natural curiosity can't run out, but it can get buried under layers of routine, busyness or disappointment. This chapter is intended to help us dig beneath the surface and communicate with loved ones in a deeper, more meaningful way.

~~~~~~

Relationships are eternal. Letting them stagnate goes against our true nature, because God imbues us with sufficient curiosity to last a lifetime. Our natural curiosity can't run out, but it can get buried under layers of routine.

~~~~~~

Remember the story about the restoration of Rembrandt's painting *The Night Watch*? Normally, museum goers spent no more time with the masterpiece than they would in the drive-through at McDonald's. But when offered a new way to interact with the painting, their attention was riveted, and they lingered over small details that had previously gone unnoticed. Their natural curiosity was rekindled. In the same way, you can still find another person fascinating whether you've been married for three months or thirty years. Whatever you think you know, there is still so much more to learn about a parent, a child or an old friend.

We communicate with one another on many levels. Sometimes, the way we connect can actually cut off curiosity; we become as perfunctory with our loved ones as we are with casual acquaintances. If we look closely at how we communicate, we can find opportunities to expand our curiosity and in so doing, deepen the relationship. *Cliché* is the first level of interaction. You bump into a slight acquaintance and exchange pleasantries: "Hi, how are you?" "Just fine, how about yourself?" There are times when this level suffices. Common courtesy dictates you ask the question, with the expectation the response will demand little of you. Most of us would become annoyed or impatient if the other person launched into a blow-by-blow account of his last two surgeries. We're not really curious about the other person; we simply want to acknowledge him or her in a pleasant way.

The second level is *fact*. "Can you tell me the time?" "Can I get directions downtown?" "I got an A on my test." "Sorry I'm late—I got stuck in traffic." Our intent is to solicit or convey specific information, with minimal feeling or emphasis. Strangers and those with a nodding acquaintance converse comfortably at the cliché and fact levels.

What's unfortunate is that loved ones often gravitate to cursory conversation as well, limiting themselves to reciting the day's events, assigning tasks and working out schedules. People bonded by blood or marriage often wind up sharing nothing more significant with one another than they would with the checkout clerk at the supermarket. Take that couple at the restaurant. Their conversation contained nothing but facts: what to order, the doneness of the filet, the soccer schedule. What could have been a special time was just another time. It was just dinner.

If we maintain communication at superficial levels, we maintain only the illusion of a happy marriage or partnership. We risk little, including finding out where we differ from one another, or where our deepest passions lie. We may avoid fights; we'll seldom feel painfully upset. But we never deeply feel love, either—and neither will our partner.

Some people communicate similarly with God. Prayer is recited, the Lord is petitioned, but there's no communion, no openness to receiving guidance, no sense of partnership. We might as well be asking God for directions downtown.

Level three is *opinion*. "Do you like me in this dress?" "Who do you think will win the election?" "That boss of mine is such a jerk." Cliché and fact are easily shared, but offering an opinion carries risk. Our opinion might be rejected or criticized. Recently, I was behind a pair of teenagers at a pizza parlor on what I surmised was their first date. The fellow asked his date to select some pizza toppings, and she responded, "What do *you* want?" He said, "Do you like pepperoni? Or is Canadian bacon better? Maybe just cheese?" She fidgeted, twirling a lock of hair with her finger, finally responding, "Well, what do *you* want?"

I could imagine her thinking: "If I say pepperoni and he wants cheese, he'll never call again." Similar thoughts must have been running through his mind.

If we don't risk stating our minds, we never express what's in our hearts. We live only at the surface of the relationship, fretting about looking bad or saying something wrong. We see no further than the surface. For a relationship to grow, we've got to get past ordering the pizza.

After thoughts comes *feelings*. Opinions convey what's going on in your head; feelings convey the heart. There's no right or wrong way to feel, but loved ones sometimes correct feelings the way an English teacher corrects grammar. How often have you shared feeling sad or depressed about a particular circumstance in your life, only to have someone gently reprimand your honest emotion? "Don't feel sad about that. Look on the bright side."

When single people express their loneliness, married friends inevitably say, "Don't worry. You'll meet someone." When a woman I know, Jill, spoke longingly of missed companionship after her divorce, a well-meaning friend told her, in an ever-so-slightly-berating tone, about an acquaintance of hers whose husband had died of cancer, leaving his wife to raise three small children alone. "Someone else's misery is supposed to comfort me? Or is she saying I shouldn't complain?" Jill wondered. "Why am I even bothering to tell her how I feel?"

"At least *her* husband didn't leave voluntarily!" Jill shot back. And the distance in the friendship became just a little bigger.

When we send the message "Don't feel that way! I'll tell you how you should feel!" the other person often pulls back, reverting to a lower, less vulnerable level of communication. Why risk exposing a part of yourself that someone else won't accept?

If we've tapped into our natural curiosity, however, we want to know exactly how our loved one feels. How that person feels matters far more than how we think he or she should feel. We listen without judging, offering advice only if requested. To be entrusted with the deeper feelings of another is a great honor, so we learn to create a safe environment where any emotion can be freely expressed. Absent that environment, communication falters.

We set our loved ones up for a fall anytime we assume that our feelings are transparent. My husband considers our home his sanctuary. While my ministry and speaking schedule keep me frequently in the company of groups of people, Ed cherishes our time alone at home. I know this because he's shared his feelings with me. Accordingly, I plan dinner parties with my girlfriends when my husband's out of town. Had he chosen to remain silent, he might go upstairs and sulk whenever I had guests, leaving me to wonder what I'd done to upset him. In turn, he could resent me, thinking, "If Mary really cared, she'd know how I feel about having company over when we have so little time to ourselves." No, I wouldn't know. If we don't express our needs, the other person is left to guess.

Expressing deep feelings can be frightening at first, but we were nervous learning to walk, too. Sometimes we stumbled, but the reward more than merited the risk. The famous French performer Maurice Chevalier once said that the best advice he ever received was "Don't be afraid to be afraid."

That doesn't mean, however, that we should blurt out our innermost feelings in the heat of the moment, whenever the mood strikes. Sometimes we set ourselves up for rejection by choosing the worst possible time to share our feelings. If we're feeling neglected by a busy spouse, it's not ideal to communicate that distress an hour before he or she goes into a critical business meeting. Yet we do it anyway. The ensuing rebuff reinforces our feeling of neglect. In case there was any doubt, the other person can now safely be labeled a thoughtless jerk, and we get to be right. If your goal is to feel good about feeling bad, fine. If you want to strengthen the relationship, however, you might ask, "Is this a good time for us to talk?" Natural curiosity doesn't grant us permission to demand answers when the other person isn't ready for a heart-to-heart. Your natural curiosity is spiritual. In wanting to know how to make a person feel cherished, the answer is that sometimes that person is best left alone, at least for the moment. Natural curiosity doesn't demand answers so much as offer love.

Spiritual curiosity also helps us choose those in whom we should confide. Obviously, intimate communication is not meant for every person we meet. I have a small circle of loved ones with whom I entrust my deepest hopes and dreams, and they entrust me similarly. We are naturally curious about one another. We respect one another and are attuned to one another's feelings.

We can pick up the phone after an absence of six months and take up right where we left off, because the connection is so strong that it transcends time and space. The people with whom we cultivate these life relationships see past our actual words and understand what we're truly trying to communicate. I remember once, depressed and frustrated over tremendous changes in our church, I called the president of our church board in tears. "Scott, I'm thinking about quitting," I told him. "There's got to be somebody better than me, someone who can handle all this pressure and dissension. I just don't think I can take it anymore!"

My friend said, "Mary, if you ever do quit, it won't be out of fear, anger or resentment. It will be out of guidance, because that's how you live your life."

I thought, "He's right." In my upset state, I had forgotten that God would assist me through all the difficult times, if only I asked for help.

Now, suppose I had confided in someone who responded, "You have every reason to quit. No one appreciates you or how hard you work." I could have moved into a very small corner of the life to which Spirit had invited me. Choose carefully with whom you share. But when you do, open up and speak from the heart.

~~~~~~~~

Choose carefully with whom you share. But when you do, open up and speak from the heart.

~~~~~~~~

Something wonderful happens when we learn to communicate our feelings with greater openness. From time to time, we break through to an even higher level—the level of *silent communion*. This is a sense of shared being. The bond is so strong, a bridge of energy runs between you, no matter if you're inches or miles apart. Call it mystical connection. Barriers disappear.

Conversation is beautiful but not required. No one has to guess what the other person thinks or feels, because it's already known. This level is the fruit of an enduring and endearing curiosity.

My friend Christy told her son that her boyfriend had invited the two of them over for dinner. "I know you're seeing your dad that night, but I just wanted you to know you were invited." Her son Alex immediately volunteered to attend the dinner party instead.

"I knew he really wanted to be with his dad. He didn't have to say so, but I know that about him," Christy said. "But I also know he thought that going to the dinner would help me. He knew that my relationship had been strained lately, and that having him there with us always lightened the mood. I'd never told him that, but he notices. So he was willing to give up what he wanted to make me happy. That he would care for me like that touched me in a way I couldn't express.

"What's amazing is, all he said was: 'I can go to dinner with *you*, Mom.' "

Christy acknowledged to him that she knew he'd been looking forward to seeing his father. Then she said, "I think I must be the luckiest mom in the world, to have a boy like you. Who could ask for more than that?"

Alex lit up, not only over his mother's praise, but because he knew he'd made her happy simply by his offer.

"Then we just cuddled. The rest of the exchange took place without our saying a word. I guess we know one another pretty well."

Love was felt and known beyond language or physical expression, which is a gift bestowed on those fluent in the language of the heart. Nothing speaks more eloquently than unspoken communication, born of curiosity, that never ceases seeking the innermost workings of the soul.

THOUGHTS THAT TRANSFORM

~ If I ever think I know everything there is to know about a loved one, I'm wrong.

~ It is my divine nature to be continuously curious.

~ When I am alone together with a loved one, I seek to know the other's thoughts and feelings, opening my own heart as well. In so doing, I will know not only my loved one better, but myself as well.

PRACTICE

During your next few dinners with a loved one, be aware of your level of communication. Do you speak in clichés? Exchange facts? Offer opinions? Express feelings? Are there any moments of silent communion?

~If the surface forms of communication dominate your interactions, consider broaching the subject without blame and asking if the other person, too, misses the closeness you once shared. For example, in the case of that couple in the restaurant, husband or wife might begin, "I don't know what's going on inside of you these days, and I miss the feeling of connection we had when we were feeling closer."

~Ask yourself: Am I doing anything to prevent my loved ones from sharing? Is it possible that I cut them off or finish their stories for them? Have I simply stopped expressing curiosity about what matters to them?

~Throughout, remember who you are. Many people in our church whom I've counseled find this exercise particularly challenging. They ask, "Why should I do something that's

*going to invite criticism? How on earth can I possibly hear
negative things about myself without feeling bad?" I explain
that it's all about choice. For instance, I can want to be the
most loving, caring mom in the world, but there will be times
when my son says, "Mom, you never listen to me. You're
always on your cell phone. Why do you want to talk to those
people more than you want to talk to me?" There are going to
be times, when my husband might say, "You've got another
business trip? Maybe we should just buy stock in the airlines.
Of course, you won't have time to spend the dividends—
you'll be off on another trip!" I'm going to be hurt. Feeling
defensive is perfectly natural. I will want to retort to my son
that my work finances his going to the college of his choice.
I'll want to remind my husband that he knew my travel
demands before he married me.*

*Practicing perfect love means that I accept those defensive
feelings as human, but also pause and remember my divine
self. I tell myself: My relationship with my loved ones means
more to me than anything else in the world. I don't want to
skim the surface. So I'm going to pause and be willing to hear
their feedback. I am going to set aside time to invite that
feedback. Defensiveness won't take me where I want to go.
Where I want to go is closer to those I love. Who I am is a child
of God. Who I'm being doesn't always reflect my true identity.
When I'm willing to communicate at a deeper level, I move
closer to my true identity, to others and to God.*

15. A Well-Guarded Secret

In my years as a minister, I've probably performed over five hundred weddings, and I believe every couple had one thing in common: They wanted the marriage to work. As I stand before the betrothed, listening to their vows, love and energy flow freely. On this most auspicious of occasions, no one is thinking, "Nice if this works out. Sure hope he doesn't leave me for his secretary." No, the newlyweds don't head down that aisle beaming with indifference. They beam with joy and hope for all the happy times ahead.

When a couple or a single parent comes to me to bless their baby, they feel the same way. They cradle the tiny body like it was the most precious thing on earth, and they're absolutely right. They cannot imagine the bond between parent and child ever severing. They don't think, "Once she's out of diapers, maybe she'll ignore everything I say. We'll scream at each other. She'll dye her hair purple and get a nose ring." No, at that moment, they think: "How wonderful to have this perfect little baby. Nothing can ever break the bond between us."

Despite the best of intentions, life happens. Careers turn demanding. Exhaustion can set in. Harsh words may be flung, sometimes at those we love most. Promises might be broken. Trust can get undermined. Feelings can get hurt. Confidences may be betrayed. Infidelity can occur. Money can get mishandled.

Tempers aren't tempered, and hurt may wedge itself between people who expected to always stay close.

What became of our marvelous relationship? Can we ever recapture our dreams?

Somewhere between the passion and the television, the cooing and the cold stares, communication often breaks down. We start speaking in shorthand, assuming that our loved ones know precisely how we feel. Often, they do not. Children may fear confiding their mistakes to their parents. Spouses stop confiding in one another. Avoidance and mistrust replace open communication.

I like to think that my daughter and I have always enjoyed a phenomenal relationship. As the lone girl amid three brothers, Jenny grew up in a world of Tonka trucks, action figures and wrestling. Early on she learned that she would have to hide her favorite dolls to protect them from being sent to the battlefield, where they were inevitably the first casualties. Louder and messier, the boys disdained Jenny's taste in television shows and interest in hairstyles. But Jenny always stood up for herself and never hesitated to speak her mind—loudly, in order to be heard—and cheerfully joined in her brothers' sports, since it seemed unlikely they would ever share her fondness for ballet.

These days, I marvel over the adult Jenny, a strong, independent and talented woman who continues to stand up for herself. Our time together is more limited now, as Jenny is married with a child of her own. My work frequently takes me out of the country, but we try to talk several times a week. One time, I was at the airport, on my way to a conference, when my cell phone rang. Jenny was calling to wish me luck on my trip.

"By the way, Mom," she added, "since you're at the airport, go to the newsstand and pick up a copy of *Dance Magazine*."

"Why?" I asked.

"You'll see," she said, her voice mysterious. "Just promise me you'll get a copy. It's important."

Curious, I scoured the small kiosk near my gate for *Dance*, without any luck. With my flight about to board, I reminded myself to check the newsstands when I landed.

Then I forgot.

A week after returning home, I was visiting my mother, who immediately plunked a copy of the latest issue of *Dance* in my lap.

"Did you see?" she asked excitedly, flipping the magazine open to a photograph of a professional jazz troupe. There, near the center, was my daughter. Her smile beamed from the page. She looked like the image of grace in her leotard, posing for a story about modern dance in America.

I couldn't have been prouder. "Isn't she the most perfect young woman you've ever seen?" I asked my mom. "Anyone looking at her could just see that she is beautiful inside and out." Mom naturally agreed, and the co-presidents of the Jenny Fan Club continued their reverie for several minutes.

The next week flew by in a whirl of meetings, speeches, ministering and the usual number of crises that crop up in the running of a large church organization. Every night, I fell into bed tired, but knowing I had made a difference. Jenny and I hadn't spoken since I'd left on my trip, which was unusual for us.

Finally, my daughter called. That warm, special relationship I mentioned earlier? Let's just say anyone eavesdropping on our conversation at this moment would think that my prior description was the product of a wishful imagination.

"I need to tell you something," she said, her voice dripping icicles. "A month ago I asked you to look at *Dance Magazine*. You knew it was important to me, and I never heard back from you. Why didn't—?"

I cut her off, greatly relieved. "Oh, honey, I did see your photograph. Grandma had a copy of the magazine. I was so proud. You should have heard me go on and on about how wonderful you are."

"But how *could* I have heard?" she asked. "How can I know what you think or what you say about me if you don't even bother to *tell* me?"

Jenny was absolutely right. *Tell* me. *Show* me. While I was grateful that my daughter felt safe enough with me to say, "Ouch! That hurt!" the situation heightened my awareness of how easily we can let the most important of relationships slide.

When I failed to give her the acknowledgment she needed, my daughter felt compelled to muse, "Maybe everything else Mom has going is more important than me!" Despite our closeness, despite all the wonderful times we've shared, Jenny is not immune to feelings of rejection. She is human, and our human nature makes us vulnerable to slights and tries to protect us from hurt.

Had Jenny remained silent, I might have gone on thinking everything was just fine; but the next time I fell short, Jenny would have more readily interpreted it as a deliberate slight. She'd have rebuffed me, and I'd have backed off, bewildered, hurt and less likely to reach out the next time.

Whenever trouble arises in a relationship—and it always does—it's as if we're at an intersection where two paths diverge. The most commonly trod path is that of human nature. It's the path that points the way to avoidance and resentment. It's the path that leads to mistrust. We follow this path naturally, because these emotions are part of our human nature. When someone does something that we perceive as hurtful, it makes perfect sense to us to feel hurt, and perhaps to begin piling on a few more negative emotions as well.

I can tell you that while Jenny studied dance at college, she never took a course on suspecting her mother of not caring. I never checked a book out from the library called *Ways My Daughter Tries to Hurt Me*. But had that scenario been played out, we would both have been acting totally human. We would have been doing what came naturally. At no point would we ever have loved each other less in our hearts, but the reality is that we would have appeared less loving, and that's really all it takes to damage a relationship.

We think of love as the warmth, passion and caring we feel for another person. But love isn't merely a feeling; it's an active verb.

~~~~~~~~~~

We think of love as the warmth, passion and caring we feel for another person. But love isn't merely a feeling; it's an active verb.

~~~~~~~~~~

The way we feel about one another is not meant to be a well-guarded secret. Saying "I love you" to a spouse or child each morning is a single syllable but a world away from "Good-bye"! Speaking from the heart takes so little—instructing a child to clean his room or to do her homework takes considerably more effort—yet often the words we most want to hear or say are the ones that go unspoken.

Virtually every person with whom I've shared Jenny's story immediately responded with a story of his or her own.

~I know a woman who felt unloved by her mother. Then one day, the older woman's caregiver called to ask a question and happened to mention how her employer talked nonstop about her wonderful daughter. The daughter was stunned. All she ever heard her mother do was complain. Thereafter, the caregiver began phoning the daughter with weekly reports singing the younger woman's praises.

~I know a man whose father never articulated a kind word to his son. Yet he framed the notes the son had written for his mother's eulogy and hung them in the living room.

~I know a woman whose young son worshiped his first-grade

teacher. After the teacher retired, he continued to bring cards and presents to her home. "It means so much to know that I had a student who thinks so much of me," she said to him one day. The boy was surprised. "All the kids think you're great," he said. But she didn't know that, because he was the only one demonstrating his feelings.

~ I know a woman who was on the verge of leaving her husband because she felt so unappreciated. "How can you not know that you mean the world to me?" he asked her. "I thought I meant nothing, because you said nothing," she responded.

One of the most tragic consequences of words left unspoken dominated headlines in the late 1990s. You may recall reading about a young woman named Amy Grossberg. Due to a shame we shared, I know that I'll never forget her.

It was more than three decades and a cultural eon ago that I was confronted with the same dilemma as Amy: Both of us were pregnant teenagers from privileged backgrounds who sought to hide our secret. I remember being shunned by the very students who had elected me Homecoming Princess and being barred from returning for my senior year by my suburban high school. When I revealed the pregnancy to my parents, it broke their hearts. But this is where the University of Delaware freshman and I diverged.

Amy and her college boyfriend, Brian Peterson, Jr., never told their parents about the pregnancy and went to a fatal extreme to hide the birth. The headlines outraged a public that had long thought itself shockproof. An attractive couple from suburban New Jersey, the two were trying to hide Amy's pregnancy when they went to the Comfort Inn in November 1996. Grossberg gave birth to a son, and the couple panicked. The next day, the baby was found dead in the motel Dumpster, its skull crushed. The former high school sweethearts served time for manslaughter before being released from prison in the year 2000.

From the initial discovery of the tiny body to the couple's sentencing, the tenor of the news stories was one of bewilderment. How could these youngsters from two well-to-do families engage in such a heinous and desperate act? The implication of the question was that money automatically begets reverence for human life. Designating a tax bracket in which morality is expected will not prevent such tragedies. But loving communication can.

Telling my parents at age sixteen that I was pregnant was the hardest thing I've ever done, but my mother and father made sure I knew that they valued me no less because of my mistake. My heart went out to Amy's parents, as I imagined them wondering what they could have done to ensure that their daughter would feel safe confiding in them. The public, the media—we were all hard on the parents of Amy Grossberg and Brian Peterson. How could they not know? Couldn't they see something was wrong? According to one report I read, a psychiatrist said that Amy wanted to avoid disgracing her family. "Amy knew her parents saw her as perfect, and she just couldn't break that image for her mom," he said. Hiding her pregnancy made perfect sense to Amy.

We must tell our children that we love them, and will continue to love them, no matter what. Even the best-intentioned parents often assume their children know they are cherished, but do the children really know? We must say the words they most need to hear. We do not have to condone everything our kids do, but they need to know we would never condemn them.

Amy Grossberg and Brian Peterson must have felt their lives would be over if their secret were found out, when in fact, their lives and that of their child would have been just beginning. We may never know for sure why this young couple chose to end their child's life, but it is easy to imagine that their vision of the future was so despairing that no glimmer of hope could squeeze through. There was no place for trusting a parent, no room for a baby to thrive.

When I first read this news story, I took the opportunity to reinforce my relationship with my own children. I asked myself, *Do they know my love is unconditional, or do I merely assume that they do? Do I sometimes get so busy that I miss opportunities to demonstrate that love?*

~~~~~~~~~

Partnering with God means harnessing our Divine resources, never letting a day go by without putting love first.

~~~~~~~~~

I think often of a family in our church whose twenty-one-year-old son was hit by a car. Sitting with the parents shortly after they received word of his death, I was struck by how they spoke of their relationship with their son. They had missed no opportunities for loving. Through their tears, they recounted memory after memory of the rich, rewarding times they had spent as a family. The parents spoke of camping trips and family dinners and visits and phone calls late into the night. They spoke about the embraces they had shared. With this child, no arguments went unresolved, no loving words were left unspoken.

We all live with the expectation that our children will outlast us, even though that's not always the case. As much as that mother and father long to wrap their arms around this boy, that isn't theirs to do anymore. Their grief over his physical loss is staggering, but there is no grief over missed opportunities, because this is a family that loves well.

They grieve the loss of a future that can never be, but they do not suffer the added heartbreak of a love not shared in the past. No pain is greater than the knowledge that we threw away a chance to love.

We are spiritual beings having a human experience. At times

our human nature can lead us to avoid, hide, mistrust and withhold the words we most need to say. If your parents never said, "I love you," human nature may carry on its tradition, no matter how much it hurts. Human nature may hang a "Do Not Disturb" sign on your neck, then feel slighted when others stay away.

But we have another side of our nature that is Divine. This side doesn't care who was wrong or right or who apologized first last time. The Divine side never assumes that others know how we feel. Partnering with God means harnessing our Divine resources, never letting a day go by without putting love first.

THOUGHTS THAT TRANSFORM

~ What often makes sense to my human nature may not be in harmony with my Divine nature.

~ I choose to put my relationships first, saying the words that most need to be said.

~ I know how much I love the people closest to me in my life, but my knowing is not as important as their knowing.

~ My word is my wand. It is a tool of magic that I can wave to wither a relationship or use to develop and declare my love.

PRACTICE

~Say the words. Tune in to the love you feel and from that place frequently tell your partner, children, friends: "I love you." Let them know the difference they make in your life.

~*When my husband and I get upset with one another, we use a phrase that reminds us how we truly want to feel. One of us says: "Let's have do-overs." Sounds silly, but we're cultivating our connection, remembering that if feeling hurt can happen in an instant, so, too, can feeling love. Hurt feelings and anger lead you to a power moment. You can increase separation or claim closeness. You can choose to proceed farther down the road that leads to resentment or avoidance, or you can decide to do something better. For us, just saying the words "Let's have do-overs" reminds us that we don't want to go down that bumpy road. We make the necessary apologies. Then, we do the do-over. We don't rehash the argument. Instead, we ask one another, "If we weren't angry right now, what would we be doing? What would we be talking about?" And that's what we talk about.*

~*Ask yourself: What opportunities am I missing to express love? The greatest grief we can experience is knowing we had moments that we failed to use well.*

~*Ask your child: Would he or she come to you with news of an unplanned pregnancy or any other type of serious problem? If the answer is "No," or "I don't know," you have a place to begin working on your relationship. Those who trust that others believe in them feel free to be open.*

~*Instill in your children these three messages:*
- *I love you, no matter what.*
- *Everybody makes mistakes.*
- *There is no mistake too big to deal with, if we face it together.*

16. Living the Truth

I once told my friend Arun Gandhi that I couldn't imagine sitting down to dinner every night with one of the great icons of the twentieth century. "What was it like having Mahatma Gandhi for a grandfather? How you must have been influenced growing up with a hero like that in the family," I said to him.

"Of course, my grandfather was a hero," he said. "But when I was a teenager, the person who ultimately set me on the path to wisdom and truth—the person who had the most profound impact—wasn't Mahatma Gandhi.

"It was John Wayne," he said, with a twinkle in his eye.

Arun grew up in the South African countryside, just north of the city of Durban. Sugarcane plantations dominated the landscape. The nearest neighbors lived two miles away. Isolated as they were from city life, Arun and his two sisters jumped at every opportunity to go to town. Durban held friends, excitement, even a movie theatre. One Saturday, Arun's father, Manilal, had a conference in the city and asked his son to drive him. His dad instructed the boy to pick up the family's groceries and take the car to a garage for an oil change.

As Arun dropped off his father at the conference, he was told: "At five o'clock in the evening, I will wait for you at this intersection. Come here and pick me up and we'll go home together."

"Fine," said Arun, who ran his errands as quickly as possible, leaving the car at the service station. Then he headed straight for the nearest movie theatre, for a John Wayne double feature. Arun idolized John Wayne. Slight of build and soft-spoken like his father and grandfather, Arun found The Duke's deep, commanding voice and looming stature the epitome of masculinity. So engrossed was the boy in *Rio Grande* that he failed to note the time. When the second movie ended, his watch read 5:30 P.M., and Arun ran all the way to the garage to fetch the family car. By the time he reached the conference center to meet his father, Arun was almost an hour late.

As he pulled up to the curb, he saw his father pacing, clearly worried for his son's safety. Now, if your teenager, who has just received his license, disappears with the car, you, too, may grow worried and anxious. But suppose your last name is Gandhi, and your family lives in exile under constant threat of death or kidnapping. Imagine how a parent might feel then. "Why are you late?" Manilal demanded.

Arun, who understood his father's anxiety and knew just how badly he'd messed up, saw a possible way out. He lied. "The car wasn't ready. I had to wait for it," he said, not realizing that his father had called the garage nearly an hour earlier.

For a moment, his father was silent. Then he spoke, very slowly. "There must be something very wrong in the way I have brought you up that would cause you to lie to me. I've got to find out where I went wrong with you.

"And in order to do that," he said, "I am going to walk home. I need this time to think. Go ahead and take the car."

"But . . ."

Nothing Arun said could change his father's mind. As dusk began to fall, the older man began his journey on foot. Home lay beyond the paved roads of the city, through a stretch of cane fields and beyond. Home was eighteen miles away.

"I couldn't leave him there and drive off," Arun said. "So for five and a half hours, I crawled behind him with the headlights on. He walked through the sugarcane, along dirt roads. His trousers became torn and caked with mud. He would slow down when he tired, but he never stopped. And he never once looked back at me. All I could do was illuminate his path so he wouldn't stumble and fall in the dark.

"As I watched my father go through all that pain and agony for a stupid lie that I told, I decided there and then that I was never going to lie again."

The vivid image of his father trekking through the dark and silent fields has never left Arun. "I wonder, if he had given me the conventional punishment that we give our children—you're grounded; no television for a week—would I have learned what he endeavored to teach me?

"Or would I have shrugged my shoulders and said, 'This time I got caught. Next time I'll make sure I don't.' Most of the time, we have the latter response. People take the punishment and go on doing the same thing over and over again, because they're not really altered by the experience."

Arun was altered. Until that time, he knew that his father loved him, but never before had he understood the true meaning of that love, the lengths to which his father would literally travel to underscore the importance of their relationship.

~~~~~~

Until that time, he knew that his father loved him,
but never before had he understood the true
meaning of that love, the lengths to which his father
would literally travel to underscore the
importance of their relationship.

~~~~~~

If our child behaves in a manner contrary to the values we have instilled, do we respond in a way that's convenient or seize an opportunity to deepen the relationship? Sometimes it feels easier to respond halfway, discouraging problems rather than encouraging greatness. Arun learned that living the truth meant something more than an absence of lying. The truth manifested in his father's willingness to pay a price in order that his son might learn. The truth also shone in the fact that Arun's father trusted his son; he trusted that Arun would in fact learn by this call to his highest nature.

As the head of the M. K. Gandhi Institute of Nonviolence, which promotes peace throughout the world, Arun has devoted his adult life to living the truth.

We, too, can live the truth through our relationships. Living in truth means practicing rigorous honesty with ourselves, God and others. Living the truth takes us beyond what I call "cash-register honesty"—that is, the kind of honesty we practice by returning the extra change the grocery store clerk accidentally hands us.

Yes, refraining from lying or cheating, and calling attention to mistakes made in our favor are important aspects of living an honest, honorable life. But there's a difference between squaring mistakes and really making truth the benchmark for our dealings with every person in our life.

There's a difference between squaring mistakes and really making truth the benchmark for our dealings with every person in our life.

Consider one of the most enduring sacred acts in our society: the oath. An oath is a pledge by which a person swears, affirms or acknowledges that he or she is bound due to religion or some other reason to perform an act faithfully and truthfully. Oaths are taken by witnesses in judicial proceedings, public officers who promise to perform their official duties faithfully, new citizens in the naturalization process and professionals such as physicians who pledge to conduct themselves according to the principles of their profession. Lying under oath is a crime. In a judicial proceeding, witnesses place their left hand on the Bible and raise their right hand, repeating the words: "I do solemnly swear that the testimony I am about to give will be the truth, the whole truth and nothing but the truth."

Living "nothing but the truth," we practice rigorous honesty with every person we encounter, from our child to our employer to the stranger on the street. Jesus said, "If you abide in My word, you shall know the Truth, and the Truth will set you free." He was saying that by developing a relationship with God, we learn to find our internal truth meter, our capacity to discern what is authentic. The truth we come to embody is knowing that God is greater than any challenge before us. When we grow beyond merely believing these words intellectually, and let them guide our behavior, we are freed from the tyranny of fear, anxiety and worry. Some of us are so fearful that we dare not risk creativity in relationships. Our limited lives constitute a lie, because we are telling ourselves, "This is the best I can do," when deep down we know better. We know that God has something greater in store for each of us, but we must stop holding back and start participating.

At one time or another, in the course of every relationship—with our parents, partner, children, neighbors, friends or coworkers—we're going to struggle with the truth. We will feel angry or hurt or betrayed. When those moments come, we can stop and practice deeper honesty: Am I responding out of fear or love? Do I want revenge or do I want the relationship to prosper?

When we think fearfully, we leave God out, narrowing possibilities. We try to find the answers on our own, and on our own, we cannot. Nobody's intellect is sufficiently developed to hold all the answers. But with God, all things are possible, including overcoming whatever problem you face. Ask yourself honestly: What is the truth; what is the God thought here?

~~~~~~~~

When we think fearfully, we leave God out, narrowing
possibilities. We try to find the answers on our own,
and on our own, we cannot.

~~~~~~~~

As I have learned from personal experience, sometimes the truth is the last thing we want to hear. In the first chapter, I shared challenges I faced with my future stepson after Ed and I became engaged. You may have surmised from my story that the relationship with Michael's father was a fairy-tale courtship.

This would not be entirely accurate. As is often the case in relationships, one person knows before the other that the two are meant to be together. In this case, I was way ahead of Ed. He and I had been dating about eight months when he began backing off. The cards, the flowers, the fabulous visions he spun for our future cropped up less frequently, and then not at all. I, on the other hand, had our future planned. I wanted a committed relationship. I wanted marriage, to build a family life together.

Ed wanted a part-time girlfriend. He wasn't ready. He was just getting his life in order. He'd had one marriage and it hadn't worked out. He didn't want to fail again. He wanted to be sure.

The more determined I grew to move forward, the more he hesitated. When virtually all your energy goes toward deciding if you even want the relationship, there's little energy to devote toward moving ahead. I began noticing that even when we were together, Ed didn't seem as present. Instead of his hanging on my every word as he once had, I found, I had to repeat myself.

"I'm confused," he'd say, and I rolled my eyes.

Praying for guidance, I asked, "What is the truth here?"

I sensed that the time had come for me to stand in the truth of what I wanted, even if that meant I had to end the relationship. Fear can make discerning the truth more difficult. I was forty-four years old, and fear made me worry, "Maybe I'm not going to meet someone else. Maybe this is my last chance and I'm throwing it away. I really don't want to spend my life without a mate. Could that actually happen to me?"

But the truth was that I needed to be myself. Who I am is not a doormat. Who I am is not a woman willing to pretend that commitment doesn't matter. Who I am is not a woman willing to wait an eternity for someone else to decide he might want what I do.

Staying in a relationship that wasn't building what I wanted to build—a life together—denied the truth. Would I eventually turn bitter and resentful? That wasn't me either. Pretending that casual dating was fine by me was virtually living a lie.

The most important relationship I needed at that time was the one with myself. If I wasn't true in that relationship, then everything else would be a sham.

~~~~~~~~~~

The most important relationship I needed at that time was the one with myself. If I wasn't true in that relationship, then everything else would be a sham.

~~~~~~~~~~

"I'm sorry, but I can't do this anymore," I told Ed. "I can no longer be just a part-time girlfriend when I deeply want so much more. I want to create a life together, to bring our families together. I want to spend the rest of my life loving you fully. But this 'part-time' life is not fulfilling to me. I need to let you go."

The month following our breakup was torturous and lonely. I dialed Ed's number so many times in my mind; I'm surprised the phone didn't actually ring on his end. But I also had a growing feeling of inward security, knowing that I was being true to myself. I had followed my heart, even if my heart was breaking.

Then Ed called. "We are so good together," he began tentatively.

"Yes," I interrupted, sobbing, "but we're *not* together."

"Well," he said, "I don't want to live my life without you. Give me just a few weeks to settle some things."

Six weeks later, Ed proposed.

I have known many people who have faced the same challenge. In every situation in which half of a couple has sublimated his or her needs, compromised the truth of what he or she wanted in order to hold on to another person, the relationship ultimately fell apart. When we are less than ourselves—a creative, loving child of our gracious, loving Creator—the foundation upon which the relationship is built inevitably crumbles.

I have known many people who made a decision for truth and said good-bye, as I did. Often, minus the demand or pressure for commitment, the other individual could more clearly discern his or her own truth. Sometimes, the end means togetherness, as it has for Ed and me. Sometimes, the relationship simply ends. Had Ed not come around, I would have been devastated, but so much less than had I managed to reel him in for a time by living a lie. Regardless of the outcome of our relationship with another person, we fool ourselves in thinking that we can find genuine fulfillment if we're less than honest.

I've always wanted the same kind of loving relationship that my parents share. They've been happily married for more than sixty years, and I've often asked them their secret. How can they have remained so in love all these years? What makes them still hold hands and gaze lovingly into one another's eyes after waking up together for over six decades?

What they told me is that they made a decision for the truth early on in their marriage; in fact, they were tested the morning after they arrived home from their honeymoon. My mom arose at 4 A.M. to make Dad a big country breakfast. She grew up on a farm, where mornings meant biscuits and gravy and pancakes and eggs and sausage and juice and coffee. (As you can see, the Thanksgiving dinner that made me feel like a Butterball came from a long tradition of family feasts.) To Mom, breakfast is the most important meal of the day.

"Your dad had to go to work that morning, so I had the whole meal laid out for him," my mom recalled, "and he took one look at all that food and said, 'I don't eat breakfast,' and left.

"And I had all the mess to clean up!"

Feeling thoroughly unappreciated, my mom angrily began shoving breakfast down the drain. Then she stopped herself and asked, *What is the truth here? The truth is that I know my husband doesn't love me one little bit less because he didn't eat his breakfast. The truth is, all I want is for us to love one another, and we do.*

While doing the dishes, she started thinking, *Why didn't I ask him what he would like to have for breakfast? It would have saved me all this trouble if I had just asked him.* She thought, *I just need to learn how to communicate better.*

At work that day, my dad started thinking: *You jerk! Why didn't you just eat the breakfast she made for you? Why didn't you just eat the food to let her know how much you love her?* He told me: "Over the years, I have thought that the first breakfast she ever made for me, I walked away from. And I've practiced never walking away from love again."

Whenever I hear my parents tell this story, I marvel at their successful prescription for six decades of living and loving together. Neither one of them blamed the other: You *should have done something different.* They both thought the truth: that they loved one another, and that nothing was more important than that. They each thought: *I could have done something different.* As my mother washed the dishes, she thought: *You know what? I didn't even ask him. I could have reached out differently.*

He thought: *I could have reached out differently.*

Six decades of living in truth has created the abundant fruit of the love they experience today.

~~~~~~

Thoughts That Transform

~ The next time I start to think, "Why didn't *you* do this differently?" I can stop and recognize my own responsibility and ask myself, "Why don't *I* do this differently?"

~ I know the difference between refraining from lies and living the truth. Not committing lies falls short of committing to the truth. The truth is when my outside life matches my inside feelings.

~ When I ask God, "What is the truth here?" the answer may not always please me, but it will always lead to a state where I can live in love.

~ Jesus said that the greatest commandment is to love God, my neighbor and myself. I cannot leave myself out of the equation.

Practice

You are equipped with an inner "truth meter," because you are connected to God, the source of all Truth. If you're a parent, you've put that truth meter to use when your kids were small and told small fibs. Something in you knew when they were telling the truth and when they were not. When you take the time to ask, that same something will respond to a question about your own life. Take a deep breath and ask, "What is the Truth in regard to _____?" Then listen for your inner knowing to respond. Gandhi said that the truth speaks to every person on the planet every day. A Course in Miracles *says that the voice for God is as loud as our willingness to listen.*

Engage in this practice at least three times a day. Asking for the truth affords you the chance to practice perfect loving. Internal conflicts often arise. Let's say you and your partner planned to attend a movie, but he or she comes home from work exhausted, barely saying a word. It's natural to feel disappointed. But when you ask, "What is the truth here?" you'll recognize: "The truth is, I'm disappointed about our date. But the bigger truth is, my opportunity to live in love does not depend on a movie."

TRANSFORMING DIFFICULT RELATIONSHIPS

SPIRITUAL PRINCIPLE
Love knows no boundaries. In opening your heart
to those you find difficult, you open yourself to a
love that emerges no other way.

*The holiest place on earth is where an
ancient hatred has turned into a present
love.*

— A Course in Miracles

17. BEYOND TOLERANCE

When Pat placed her mother in a nursing home, she confided to a sympathetic staff member, "This woman is not my favorite person."

The feeling seemed mutual. Whenever Pat visited her mother—about once a month, if that—Josephine would wheel herself over to the television and flip it on. When the two did sit face-to-face, Josephine would shake her finger and spew syllables at her daughter. Pat understood her mother's anger: Josephine was frustrated by her stroke. And she was mourning her husband. Josephine had hardly spent a night away from Pat's father in more than forty years of marriage. Now, her husband was gone, and she could no longer care for herself.

With the stroke slurring her speech and her husband's death sapping her spirit, Pat's mother lost all hope. The only time she left her room was to get her hair done down the hall or to see the doctor. Although Josephine and Pat had never been close, it hurt Pat to see this once vibrant, energetic woman wasting away in a chair, her every day as monotonous as the last.

Her family should not have come to this, Pat thought. But then again, life in her household had always fallen far short of idyllic. In fact, while growing up in the '60s, Pat used to fantasize that Donna Reed was her mother. She imagined sitting at the kitchen table, sharing confidences about boys and hairstyles with the glamorous but insightful Donna.

"My own mother and I rarely discussed anything more intimate than the weather report," Pat said. "Ours was not a family of warm embraces and cocoa around the fireplace. Mom was totally focused on Dad, who could be kind, gentle and loving, and then, without warning, erupt in an alcoholic rage. I adored my father when he was sober and blamed my mother when he was not, because she didn't do anything to protect me."

The wedge between mother and daughter was formed early on, widening with age. Thus, nursing home visits consisted of Pat reciting her children's activities, followed by a half hour of *Jeopardy!* Then Pat would drive home.

One day, Pat was sorting through the boxes of her mother's belongings that had been left at her parents' house. Inside a carton of still-wrapped linens purchased in Europe, Pat found a note from her mother that read: "Hi, honey. I thought these would look good on your table."

"How odd," Pat thought. "Why did she buy me these beautiful linens, then not even tell me about the gift?"

Much to Pat's astonishment, other boxes held similar treasures. A safety-deposit box contained a small jewelry case with a one-carat diamond inside. "I bought you this because I know you always wanted one," read the accompanying note.

Clearly, Josephine had intended for Pat to discover these gifts after her death. "How eerie," Pat thought. "Why?"

Then it hit her. "I realized that my mother could never have given me these items in person, fearing that I would reject her gifts. And she would have been right." That she would only feel safe expressing her feelings after her death saddened Pat beyond words.

"I wanted to go to her, but what would I say? 'Since you

bought me a diamond, I'll be the daughter you always wanted me to be'? I didn't want her to feel as if she'd somehow purchased my forgiveness."

About a week later, while attending a self-improvement seminar, Pat overheard a woman talking about her daughter: "I love her so much, I just don't understand why everything I do is wrong. Why doesn't she love me back?" With a jolt, Pat realized that woman could have been her own mother talking about her. "Wow," she thought. "Could it be that my mom loves me?"

Pat left the meeting and drove straight to the nursing home. She had no idea what to say. She and her mother had always been so unalike—the best the two had ever managed was to tolerate one another's differences. Being tolerant, thought Pat, was just another way of saying "putting up with." The idea that real love might exist somewhere beneath the surface was so overwhelming that Pat knew she could not figure out what to do on her own. Could God help?

"When it came to God, I'd always been on the fence. I believed that Higher Power worked miracles in people's lives, but not in mine," Pat said.

Maybe if she asked now, though, God could help. Pat didn't really know where to begin. The short, obligatory nursing home visits filled Pat with guilt; the years of enduring her father's rage while her mother sat by still rankled. How could she possibly reconcile the notion of this cold, estranged relationship with the image of a woman who stored linens for her daughter?

As Pat walked into the nursing home, she prayed for guidance, not knowing what to expect. Would God provide an answer? And if so, how would she know? Friends of Pat's had talked about feeling God's presence, carrying on an inner dialogue with God, but quite frankly, she hadn't paid much attention. Why learn a new language for a country you have no hope of ever visiting? Would God manifest like an apparition of

George Burns in one of those old movies? Or was this God's busy time?

Mere steps from her mother's room, Pat got an idea. It wasn't something she'd ever thought on her own. She knew instinctively that this was a message from a Higher Source. She felt as if she were reading words scrawled on her heart: "Your mother may have disappointed you, but she did the best she knew how."

Pat took a deep breath and said, "God, lead me in how to truly love my mother." She opened the door to her mother's room. Josephine wore the same dour expression and offered her usual indifferent greeting. The two women rarely embraced, and they did not do so now. For a fleeting moment, Pat was disappointed. She had expected this revelation to make her mother look different.

~~~~~~~~

She felt as if she were reading words scrawled on her heart: "Your mother may have disappointed you, but she did the best she knew how."

~~~~~~~~

Then she felt another nudge. Her mother hadn't changed, but Pat had. She took another deep breath and sat on her mother's bed, instead of in her usual chair. Then, much to the surprise of both women, she took her mother's hand, knowing instinctively that she would not be rejected. In that moment, Pat released a lifetime of resentment. Her mother had definitely made some mistakes. So had Pat. So what? Who was right and who was wrong simply no longer mattered.

"I'm sorry, Mom, for all the times I've pushed you away," Pat said. "From now on, you can count on me to be the daughter you always wanted."

Josephine squeezed Pat's hand, and with speech as clear and

precise as if the stroke had never happened, she said, "I love you, Patti."

In the past, Pat had always tuned out her mother's stories about her youth, but over the ensuing weeks, she began recalling them with awe: As a young woman, Josephine had left home in Portland to begin a new life in Washington, D.C., on her own. She had translated top-secret documents during World War II. She had learned to fly an airplane. Pat dug up old family pictures. "What am I going to do with these?" she wondered. Then an idea came: "Wouldn't Mom love to have her life story commemorated in some way?" Pat spent several hours pasting pictures to form a collage, adding a written biography to accompany the photos.

"Mom took one look at that collage, wheeled herself out into the hallway and grabbed the first staff member who came along," Pat said. "The next thing I knew, the room had filled with aides and nurses, everybody looking at the pictures."

The nursing home manager put a notice in the newsletter encouraging other families to create historical collages for their elderly relatives. The idea caught on with a chain of nursing homes, and now families in Oregon and California are making these keepsakes that celebrate the person behind the infirmity.

The snowball of goodwill felt to Pat like a nudge from God, saying, "See, you can make a difference. Don't stop here." So Pat didn't. She created a foundation, Small Hands-Big Hearts, that empowers young people in the U.S. to aid communities in other countries. She also began leading motivational seminars.

After all those years of bitterness, with help from her Higher Power, Pat's relationship with her mother became the catalyst for so much good. After all those years of bitterness, this newfound relationship paved the way for another person to step into her own greatness—and that person was Pat's mother.

For most of her life, Pat had looked at Josephine through

lenses tinted with anger. The longer she looked, the more her reality became colored. In Pat's eyes, her mother could be nothing more than an angry woman. The moment the obstructing lenses came off, Pat saw clearly an extraordinary person who wanted nothing more than for her daughter to have a great life.

Pat nourished her mother with love, and at age eighty-five, Josephine began to blossom. A world that had shrunk to the size of a wheelchair now stretched miles outside her door.

〰〰〰

Embrace differences, don't just tolerate them.

〰〰〰

First, Josephine began wheeling herself as far as her doorway, then she tentatively ventured down the hall. Her speech remained muddled, but she reached out in spite of her difficulty. Soon, she visited Pat's home. She attended her granddaughter's wedding. In time, she became what her daughter called "a social butterfly," attending the theatre and parties, going shopping.

During one visit, she handed Pat her wedding ring. Pat was shocked. Josephine had always proclaimed, "I'm going to my grave with this ring!"

Without a word, she wheeled herself across the hall and returned a few minutes later with the reason for her change of heart. Josephine introduced Pat to her boyfriend. Pat was speechless.

"I can't keep up with her," Pat said.

Then one day, shortly after Josephine came down with a virus, the nursing home called unexpectedly. "Oh no," Pat thought immediately. "We've just healed our relationship and now . . ."

No, the manager quickly assured her, Josephine was fine. She was simply calling to inform Pat that her mother had been chosen as a senior citizen Rose Festival Princess. The Rose Festival is an annual extravaganza in Portland highlighted by a nationally televised parade and the crowning of a high school Queen. Several years ago, senior citizens began being selected for their own court. As one of the honored senior princesses, Josephine attended the senior coronation, which was presided over by an Oregon congressman. A photograph of her court appeared in the local newspaper. In her new blue silk dress and pearl earrings, Josephine was a knockout.

Embrace differences, don't just tolerate them. That's the lesson Pat learned from her mother, and Pat now couldn't be prouder to be her mother's daughter.

~~~~~~

Thoughts That Transform

~ My parents did not or do not always behave the way I wanted or want but that hardly makes me unique. As Socrates said, "Parents are destined to disappoint their children."

~ I create a template for my own children through the example I set in how I think of, speak about and treat my own parents.

~ I can choose to extend love to my parents only when they conform to my wishes, or I can find the hand of God in our differences.

~ Forgiving and loving my parents has the potential to transform my life.

~ My parents did the best they knew how. I choose to focus on and be grateful for the gifts I *did* receive, not the least of which was being born. Thanks, Mom and Dad.

PRACTICE

One of the ways Pat cut through the guilt and baggage of her relationship with her mother was to create a collage. That gift not only provided joy to Josephine; it allowed Pat to see her mother from a fresh perspective, as an interesting individual, not just as "Mom." Consider making your own collage or something similar. In our congregation, many members have interviewed their parents to write oral histories, learning facts about their families they never knew before. Some of our congregants have also collected old photos to create calendars that are professionally printed at copy shops. They make two copies: one for each generation. Then, they circle an agreed-upon date each month for a get-together. At the gathering, the parent explains the story behind "the picture of the month" and what life was like at that time.

18. Raising Your Boiling Point

Let me introduce you to a *really* difficult woman. No, wait. You've already met. She's the customer service representative who hung up after keeping you on hold for twenty minutes. She's the employer who blames you for her mistakes. She's the mother-in-law who can't believe you're raising the children that way. Of course, she is just as often a he. He's the man who cut you off on the freeway, nearly causing a five-car pileup. He's the neighbor who parks his monster truck in front of your house, leaving his driveway empty. He's the former love who relishes telling everyone your secrets.

We all know difficult people. They seem to sap our energy or fuel us with rage. The sound of their voice on the answering machine can make our blood pressure rise. We think: "What does he want now?" We may find excuses to avoid the person. We're suddenly too busy to return a phone call. We avoid functions where that person will be present. Whether we know our difficult people for five minutes or fifty years, any time spent with them seems far too long.

One of my particular nemeses was a United Airlines ticket agent in Kansas City who was determined to keep me from my children just when I was missing them most.

I had inadvertently committed to speak at a conference in Kansas City the same week my kids were scheduled home from college for spring break. Fortunately, the conference wrapped up early, and I called the airport to catch the next plane so that our family could at least share one day together. The airline had one seat left on a 7:30 A.M. flight the following morning. I was thrilled. We made the necessary changes over the phone, and the agent instructed me to go straight to the gate.

The next morning, I awakened at five o'clock and headed for the airport. It was packed. Even at the gate, I had to wait in line forever. Finally, I reached the front, only to be told:

"You can't switch tickets here. You'll need to go to the ticket counter. Next, please."

"Now wait a minute," I said. "I've been in line half an hour. The woman on the phone told me to check in at the gate, NOT at the ticket counter, which is clear at the other end of the airport. I'm sure the change is in the computer. Can't you just look?"

"Can't do that. Next."

"Isn't there something—"

"You're keeping people waiting, ma'am. I can't help you. Next."

"But I'll miss my flight, and my children will only be in town for another day. Please! Besides, the woman on the phone told me that I could just come here, and now it's getting close to take-off time."

She responded: "You must not have listened very well. You should listen better."

At this point, I lost it. Thanks to this pigheaded ticket taker, I was going to have virtually no time with my children. So I gave her a piece of my mind I would have been better off keeping. I considered this woman a few fries short of a Happy Meal, which I let her know. And that was before losing my temper. Modulate my voice . . . why bother?

Finally, in defeat but still steaming, I turned to leave—and heard a voice from the line next to mine.

"Mary? Mary Morrissey? The minister from Living Enrichment Center?"

I said, "It depends. How long have you been listening to me? I'm not sure it is me."

With a face the color of an overripe chili pepper, I hiked back to the ticket counter, where the line stretched longer still. The wait gave me time to reflect. Yes, it's embarrassing to get caught in a tantrum when one makes a living preaching peace. But the very fact that I had been recognized forced me to examine my behavior when I otherwise might have remained rankled.

Kind, helpful individuals bring out our best side. Difficult people do just the opposite. A stranger observing me in a positive circumstance might think, "Doesn't she seem pleasant?" The folks at the United gate that fateful Friday morning may have selected a less flattering adjective.

The situation had turned me into a two-year-old. I wanted things my way or no way. Had I misheard the original agent? Probably not. Was the woman at the gate unnecessarily snide? No question. Did I have a right to feel upset? Absolutely. But as is so often the case with relationships, being right doesn't really matter. Being right wasn't worth diminishing myself. Being right doesn't have anything to do with practicing perfect love. In order for me to be right, somebody else has to be wrong. Right/wrong thinking only creates separation. It doesn't matter that I'd never have seen that ticket taker again. When I walk away from an angry encounter, the one I walk away with is me. And the anger stays with me.

Being right doesn't have anything to do with practicing perfect love.

Ours was a very fleeting imperfect relationship. But it provided me the opportunity to practice perfect loving.

We don't have to let circumstances determine our behavior. If we do, we'll wind up as emotional yo-yos, because, quite frankly, with all the difficult people in the world, what are the odds we'll encounter only the pleasant ones? I think that sometimes we don't want to acknowledge the existence of people unlike ourselves (we're the nice ones, of course), but there's no avoiding them. They're going to teach our children, live next door, keep us off the airplane and, yes, share our last name. Difficult people offer an opportunity for us to grow spiritually. When challenged, we're offered a choice: We can react to the moment, or we can find and draw from the Divine presence within ourselves.

We are invited to realize the tremendous influence we wield through the choices we make. Through the life of Jesus, we are provided a template for God-like behavior. It's as if He is telling us: "You want to see God? Then look at me. There is no separation here. That same Presence and Power is in you. Follow me. Follow my way of being, and you will find that Power yourself. You will do the things that I do and greater things still." Our own God-like behavior brings us closer to our true selves, as children of God.

I was sorely disappointed at missing my flight that morning, but I'm grateful that there was a congregant in my path to remind me of something more important. We may not always respond to rudeness or indifference from our highest mind. But we always have the opportunity for reflection, for turning the bad moment into a learning experience. We can remind ourselves that the difficult moment will pass, but that the person we choose to be over an accumulation of such small moments is the person we ultimately become. Someone is standing at the gate waiting to check you in. At that critical moment, we can make a choice that will send us either forward—or to the back of the line to try again.

Coping with difficult people in a loving way doesn't always

come easily. It takes practice. Certain people and circumstances can provoke knee-jerk reactions in us that take time to reverse. Think about a time you lashed out at someone: What set you off? Did you later regret your harsh words, only to respond the same way the next time?

~~~~~~

Coping with difficult people in a loving way doesn't always come easily. It takes practice.

~~~~~~

We all have knee-jerk reactions. I was listening to someone say, "You know, I don't know why but when I see someone in really nice clothes, I think, 'Wow, she's just materialistic.' And if I see somebody in old, torn or worn garments, I think, 'What a loser.' This is the way I am, but I don't know why. It's just my knee-jerk reaction."

We can automatically respond negatively to negativity, trying to pull ourselves up by bringing someone else down. But what if we partnered with God to do something better?

A woman with a voice like a foghorn yelled at Amanda after her car alarm went off. "It's so intrusive . . . There's no need to have the alarm set so sensitively . . . It was driving me crazy," and on and on about Amanda's lack of consideration for others. The incident occurred in a tourist town on a holiday weekend and actually drew a fair-sized crowd.

"Of course, she doesn't acknowledge WHY the alarm went off, which was because her car had bumped into mine. And my car was parked!" Amanda explained. "I had to clamp my hand over my mouth to hold the sarcasm in. Lungs like hers, she was quite a bit noisier than my alarm.

"I finally just snipped at her, 'I don't think my alarm is any competition for YOU! Have a nice day,' and then we drove off."

Amanda had a sudden, somewhat appealing vision of herself following the woman around town with her alarm blaring like a siren. "Then I told myself, 'That's not really who I want to be.' In a flash, the thought came to me: 'She set off the alarm in my car. Why did I let her set off the alarm inside me?' "

Amanda had to admit to herself that she, too, hates blaring car alarms. That made her partly at fault. Maybe hers *was* set too sensitively, if a tiny tap on the bumper would set it wailing. Furthermore, she realized, she needn't have matched the woman rudeness for rudeness.

What could she do? Remember that line from *A Course in Miracles*? "I must have chosen wrongly, because I am not at peace." Amanda was not at peace. She wanted to feel good in a way that lasted longer than the temporary delight of revenge. She wanted to feel good about herself.

"I'm an action-oriented person. I had to do *something*, and soon. So I kept asking myself: 'What would feel right here?' I didn't get an answer, but all that upset left me starving, so my son and I went out for dinner, where he spilled his extra-large root beer all over the table. The waitress looked exhausted, but she couldn't have been sweeter as she mopped up the mess. I thought, "Here's my answer," and promptly left a 50 percent tip, something I've never done before. Leaving that money was automatic, like a reflex. There was my new knee-jerk reaction, and it felt terrific."

If someone hurts or annoys us, we may start to react automatically; we can be conditioned to respond in a number of ways. What if we automatically turned to God? Ask: "How can I get over this and return to love?" We really know we're on a spiritual path when compassion becomes our knee-jerk reaction.

~~~~~~~

We really know we're on a spiritual path when
compassion becomes our knee-jerk reaction.

~~~~~~~

Had the woman who set off the alarm parked elsewhere, Amanda would not have had the opportunity to stretch her capacity for compassion that day. Is it possible that in the perfection of God's plan, some of our relationships are what we call "difficult"? In the soul's journey from spiritual infancy to fully manifesting Spirit in human form, do we need people who assist us in digging deeper to draw forth a loving response? God's plan encompasses all relationships, even the troubled ones. When we partner with God, difficult people can rouse us from spiritual slumber. When we stop criticizing and cringing, and start adopting a higher perspective, we tap into perfect love, which is itself greatness, regardless of the circumstance.

~~~~~~~~

God's plan encompasses all relationships, even the
troubled ones. When we partner with God, difficult
people can rouse us from spiritual slumber.

~~~~~~~~

Over the years, I have ridden many taxicabs in New York, and the drivers have always been extremely polite. Then, one day, on my way to give a speech at the United Nations, I met a driver who was not.

I hopped in the cab with my friend Dr. Michael Beckwith and spoke through the holes in the barrier separating the front and back seats. "We would like to go to the United Nations, to the Forty-sixth Street entrance," I told the driver. He was drinking something and just kept slurping from his straw. We didn't move. Maybe he didn't hear me over the slurping. So I repeated our destination, this time a little louder.

He whipped his head around, snarling, "When I want to hear where you're going, I'll ask ya!"

So I sat back and waited. He slurped his drink, slowly. After the final slurp, he said: "So, where do you want to go?"

"To the United Nations."

As he pulled out into traffic, raising his voice in an angry, accusatory tone, he said, "Hey, lady, there's four buildings there, and if you're not going to tell me which street you want to go to and what entrance, if you're going to play games with me, I'm taking you no place!"

Just like that! Here I am, prepped to deliver a speech about nonviolence, and I'm contemplating murder. Okay, not murder, but my feelings were anything but peaceful. I wanted to tell him, "Fine, I'm getting out of this cab and not paying you one dime!"

I took a deep breath and thought about my options. Yes, I felt frustrated. Taxicab drivers had always treated me kindly, and this one had lashed out for no reason. At a human level, I had every right to be upset with him. But given the nature of my speech, I thought, "How do I transform this energy?" The answer was "Do not participate in it." Once we exercise fear and make it our practice, once we try resentment and make it our habit, once we employ aggression and make it routine, those actions dominate our destiny.

I recalled how Gandhi trained people to do their work. When violence came their way, they proceeded with their task. They either went around the violence or sat still until they could move forward again, but they never participated in it. I asked myself, "How would Jesus respond? How would the Dalai Lama handle a rude taxi driver?" I imagined for a minute.

We reached the United Nations in silence. I prayed for Holy Spirit to lift me above my anger. I saw that the meter read six dollars. I opened my wallet to pay—I had a five-dollar bill, a one and a twenty. I felt a nudge that said: "Give him the twenty and tell him to keep the change." I'll tell you what I told that nudge. "Forget it! He ought to pay *us* for this ride!"

I could stiff him a tip, and he would doubtless growl even harder at the next hapless traveler foolish enough to enter his cab. Both rider and driver might pass on their foul moods to the next people they encountered. Or, I could take this moment to show compassion. The Dalai Lama says, "My religion is kindness." He isn't telling us to be kind when the mood strikes or when people treat us respectfully, but to practice our religion no matter what the circumstance.

"Give him the twenty dollars," the nudge told me again. My ego arguing, I took out the largest bill, put it through the little window in the barrier and said, "Here. Keep the change." He turned around and looked at me, and just for a second, his eyes filled halfway up with tears. "Thanks, lady," he said gruffly.

"Good-bye," I said, and got out of the cab.

Snubbing the driver would have felt delicious for about five minutes—and believe me, I was sorely tempted—but showing him compassion filled me with a euphoria that lasted hours and is still available whenever I recall the situation.

We all have to confront the rude taxi drivers, ticket takers and other strangers who can set off our alarms. While many of these people we label "difficult" may vanish from our lives in an instant, every encounter provides a fleeting moment of truth. These strangers whom we will likely never see again are put in our path for a reason: They offer us the opportunity to think about who we choose to be when the going gets tough.

~~~~~~~

There is no place where God is not, no place at all.
Even in the faces of difficult people, we can find God.

~~~~~~~

There will be tough going in our most significant relationships, and the stakes are far higher. When a loved one lashes out, what if we have conditioned ourselves to kindness? There was a very clever slogan for one of the television networks called "Must-See TV," but at the end of my life, I don't think I'll reflect, "If only I'd watched a little more television!" I may, however, look back and wish I'd been more compassionate. Why not make our knee-jerk reaction compassion, not self-defense?

There is no place where God is not, no place at all. Even in the faces of difficult people, we can find God. Difficult people are part of God's plan.

Otherwise, God would have created everyone exactly like us.

~~~~~~

THOUGHTS THAT TRANSFORM

~ It really does not matter who is right!

~ I can learn to respond with compassion instead of self-defense.

~ Sweet-tempered, helpful individuals offer me kindness; difficult people offer me the chance to grow. Difficult people—whether I spend five minutes or five decades with them—challenge me to become the person I truly desire to be.

PRACTICE

Those self-help magazine articles suggest counting to ten when you're upset. Sorry, but counting to ten is trite. Worse, the technique doesn't really work. Nor does taking a walk to cool off always do the trick. (Taking a walk out of the ticket line would have put me back at the end again, which would have really left me steaming!) Consider these steps instead:

~Take three intentional breaths. When my children were little, I would read them a book called The Great Me and the Little Me. *The "Little Me" thinks of no one but myself. The "Great Me" cares about others. To move from little to great, notice your breathing: Breathe out tension, breathe in*

relaxation. *Breathe out anger, breathe in peace. Breathe out anxiety, breathe in compassion.*

~*Invite your imagined hero to observe you.* The next time you feel annoyed or upset at someone, pretend that someone you greatly admire is looking on. Who would you want that person to see? Would your hero respond that way?

~*Remember the big picture.* Create a spiritual habit of forgiving the tiny treasons of everyday life. Resisting the temptation toward revenge in the face of smaller infractions teaches you to do the same when greater betrayals arise.

~*God as Creator said,* "Let there be light." As God's offspring, we are imbued with that same creative capacity, which means we are constantly saying, "Let there be . . ." But usually, we're unaware of the incredibly awesome power at work in us. Unconsciously, we say, "Let there be judgment; let there be criticism; let there be hostility." When you feel a bout of hurt or condemnation coming on, ask God for help. Learn this prayer: "God, I really want to see this with compassion. I want to turn this stumbling block into a stepping-stone."

19. THE CHALLENGE OF BETRAYAL

I once read a newspaper article about a man looking for a used car who saw a late-model Jaguar advertised in the classified section of the newspaper. The price: $50. He thought this surely was a misprint, but just in case, he called the number listed.

The woman who answered said, "Yes, the Jag's price is fifty dollars. You're the first person who's called."

He raced over to her house, and there sat the car. Barely a year old, with 3,500 miles on it, the Jaguar appeared in near perfect condition. Before the woman could change her mind, the fellow handed her the money. She turned over the registration of the vehicle to him without a word.

Once he had the pink slip in his hand, he couldn't help himself. He had to know. "I don't get it. Why would you sell this car for fifty dollars? Obviously it's worth thousands and thousands."

She said, "I'll tell you why. It belonged to my husband, who left me. He didn't tell me face-to-face; he left me a note saying he was in Jamaica with his girlfriend and that I could have the house, the other car and the bank accounts.

"All he wanted was that I sell his Jaguar and send him the money."

Sure, we can laugh at this story. But it strikes a chord, doesn't it? When someone betrays us, vengeance seems like a perfectly normal response. The one who pained us deserves our pain tenfold. Sometimes, we deny the hurt, refuse even to see the betrayal, which builds a wall of isolation. We can't fathom that someone would hurt us so profoundly, so, in our minds, it never happened.

But betrayal does happen. Every one of us has been betrayed. Perhaps it was a business partner who cheated, a spouse who was unfaithful or even a friend who gave away your deepest secret. The friend you could always count on got too busy for you. The promotion your boss promised went to someone less deserving. One way or another, somebody let you down, dashing your expectation so deeply that you were wounded to the core.

We expect people and circumstances to abide by certain rules, and when those rules get violated, our notions about human decency can shatter. Imagine the intense feeling of betrayal of a Vietnam veteran who witnessed unspeakable violence in the name of freedom only to return home not as a conquering hero but as a social pariah. Imagine how terrifying the world must present itself to a child who is taught to listen to and respect grown-ups only to be molested by a family member or teacher.

In the classic song "You've Got a Friend," James Taylor sings: "People can be so cold. They'll hurt you and desert you, and take your soul if you let them, oh but don't you let them . . ."

Don't you let them take your soul. One of the most formidable tasks we ever face is to take betrayal and transform it into something better. We can't stop people from lying to us and letting us down. And sometimes, I know it's hard to stop the pain from festering. We don't want to stop feeling vindictive, because there's a juicy bit of pleasure in payback. But the pleasure doesn't last. Ultimately, we wind up worse than where we started, feeling more hurt and miserable and stuck in a perpetual rerun of our worst moments.

~~~~~~~~~

One of the most formidable tasks we ever face is to
take betrayal and transform it into something better.

~~~~~~~~~

Or perhaps we think that denying a betrayal will make it go away. Facing a betrayal is very painful, but ultimately less difficult than ignoring the hurt. Pretending saps our energy—the very energy that could be used for loving.

Besides, betrayal contains within it a seed of opportunity. We can choose to reconcile the hurtful experience with what we desire most in life. And that really is not vengeance. What we want most is love. At the most profound and true level, people who have hurt us the most offer a great gift. We can learn to open our hearts and through the betrayal find entrance into an everlasting, unconditional love.

This task challenges us. To touch this love, we are required to open our hearts at the precise moment every instinct urges us to shut them down. Closing our hearts doesn't build what we want to experience. Closing our hearts traps us in our painful feelings. Closing our hearts cuts us off from the opportunity to tap into greater love.

~~~~~~~~~

We are required to open our hearts at the precise
moment every instinct urges us to shut them down.

~~~~~~~~~

You may read these words and think, "Mary's right. I can dig deep in myself and find love in a hurtful situation, but not this one. Mary meant everyone except my husband." Or mother. Or sister. Or employer. Every person, every circumstance, except the one I'm facing right now. Betrayal is undoubtedly the last experience for which we'd sign up, but the class is mandatory.

I know a woman I'll call Elaine whose husband of twenty years one day announced, "I'm in love with someone else." Worse yet, Elaine had introduced this "someone else" to her husband.

"Jan and I had met at a professional development conference and really hit it off," Elaine said. "We had daughters entering the same kindergarten class and we had similar views on public relations, the field in which we both worked. So, when an opening arose at my company, I suggested Jan to the owner, who happened to be my husband." Elaine and Jan had joined the same car pool. Their daughters had played at one another's homes. Elaine had considered Jan a friend.

"At times like this, you can choose to rise above the ugliness or go under," Elaine said. "I chose submersion."

Elaine said the treachery felt like a behemoth that crushed her with its sheer bulk. She had no desire to get up again—let alone rise above the fray. She had been doubly betrayed, by her husband and by a trusted friend. The only thing that really comforted was feeling hurt. The most natural, human response in the world when you're wronged is to wrong back. Certainly, Elaine told herself, no one deserved vindication more than she.

Vitriol tasted delicious, as Elaine began putting her public relations training to work in a new way. "We lived in a small community, and I began letting everyone know just how horribly I'd been treated," Elaine said. "At the first hint of gossip, I chimed right in." If anyone expressed interest in her life, even smiled in what she perceived to be a sympathetic manner, "out lashed my tongue about that conniving, backstabbing, home-wrecking former coworker of mine," she said. She took pains to remind other parents that she and Jan had even served as Girl Scout leaders together. Fueling this smear campaign was her unbearable sense of loss. For despite everything, she missed her husband. She also felt overwhelmed as a single parent—cooking, cleaning, shopping and mediating arguments on her own. Weekends when her children visited their father, she wanted someone to hug her. But she was all alone.

Spirituality had always struck Elaine as hokey. She was too busy getting even to bother with God. So when Jan wrote her a letter asking for forgiveness, Elaine tore it up.

But after a time, feeling wronged didn't feel right anymore. Desperate, in a moment of anguished aloneness, she cried out to God for help. There was no quick and snappy reply, but she did feel heard. Tentatively, she attended a workshop on spirituality. Like many people, Elaine was starting down a spiritual path as a means of escaping pain. But she stuck with it. She realized that she did not want to be bitter. Harboring a grudge had generated so much ill feeling in her. She's a creative person, but all her creative energy was being used up on a single negative PR campaign.

"How I wanted to show up in the world I wasn't yet sure," Elaine said, "but I knew it would not be like this."

After not speaking to Jan for over a year, Elaine called and arranged a meeting. She had prepared a little speech about how she didn't like the way Jan and Don had found one another, but how she had forgiven her and was ready to move on.

Then she opened her mouth and said something else entirely.

"Thank you."

"Thank you?" Jan repeated.

"Yes, thank you for being good to my children and to Don." The words surprised Elaine, but they were the truth. Then she apologized for spreading gossip.

Elaine felt almost as if she were floating. The heavy weight of betrayal had been lifted, and she felt as if she could accomplish anything.

A short time later, Elaine launched a new career, even returning to school to complete her master's degree. Today, she says, she lives in a kind of joy she could never have imagined during her dark time.

It may be difficult to conceive of rising above a betrayal to the degree that Elaine did. But how much more difficult it is to remain in pain. And as we develop a more personal relationship with God, we come to realize that no breach of faith is bigger than God. Opening our heart means that we refuse to let hatred, revenge or coldness find a permanent home in us. Instead, we consciously ask ourselves, "How can I see this differently? If love led my thinking, what would I think now? If love guided my actions, what would I do right now?"

~~~~~~~~

Opening our heart means that we refuse to let hatred, revenge or coldness find a permanent home in us.

~~~~~~~~

A friend, whom I will call Jeff, was divorced when his daughter, Connie, was six years old. He wanted very much to maintain a solid relationship with Connie, whom he loved deeply, but in time his wife remarried, and he began to suspect that she was trying to drive a wedge between father and daughter. Jeff was always eager to drive Connie to her soccer practice, assist with homework, arrange slumber parties—anything that would keep the two of them connected. Sometimes his daughter rejected his efforts, sometimes she accepted. But he believed that if he just kept trying, eventually Connie would let down her guard. After all, he was her dad. He loved her more than anything else in the world, and deep down, he reasoned, she must feel the same overwhelming love for him.

Then came the day when Connie called him to say: "I have exciting news." His daughter was getting married. Jeff's heart soared, because he thought, "I'm going to get to give her away. I know she's been close to her stepdad, so maybe we'll accompany her down the aisle together." He imagined this precious, powerful moment in his only daughter's life: Connie dressed in white, clinging to his arm, the eyes of the wedding guests upon them.

She began describing the plans, then hesitated and said: "I want to let you know, Dad, Roy is going to walk me down the aisle."

His daughter's words felt so sharp they could have all but carved his heart right out of his chest. The proudest moment of his life was being stolen from him. Never had he felt so betrayed. Even the divorce had not cut him as deeply as being cast out from his rightful place beside his daughter, a daughter he had offered love to her entire life.

Mistaking his silence for acquiescence, Connie went on. "But we do want you to be in the service," she said to her father. "After the vows, we want you to come up and give a blessing for us."

The blessing felt like an afterthought, a token gesture that made Jeff cringe. Obviously she felt obligated to acknowledge him in some way at the ceremony, but he wasn't sure which role felt worse: Discarded Dad or Perfunctory Parent. He wished his daughter well and hung up without expressing his feelings. Then he thought, "Enough is enough. I've tried all her life to be there for her . . ." He remembered all the times he'd sacrificed his own plans at the last minute to chauffeur her to soccer practice, loan her the car, and his sadness burned to rage.

"Let her have her way. I don't need to even be there," he thought.

Revenge tasted sweet in his mind. His absence would cast sadness over his daughter's special day, and maybe Connie would realize how wrong she'd been to shunt him off to the sidelines. Then he imagined her tears and sighed. He couldn't hurt his daughter that way. So he thought, fine, he could give the blessing, but he certainly wouldn't pretend to be overjoyed. And he wasn't going to show up at rehearsal for his measly part. Bad enough to watch the stepfather give away his little girl once; twice went beyond the call of duty. Besides, all that joy and nervous festivity would only exacerbate his own sense of loneliness and pain.

As the wedding date approached, Jeff continued to grapple

with his feelings of betrayal. He had let his daughter's rejection sap every ounce of joy from his being. Friends seemed more distant, food tasted bland, and he felt horribly alone. A voice inside him kept urging: "Don't go to the rehearsal, for heaven's sake. Enough is enough."

But Jeff is a deeply spiritual man, and in his pain, he prayed for a miracle. He prayed for God to help him feel good about his daughter's wedding. And the moment Jeff began praying, he realized that part of his loneliness stemmed from feeling separate from God's presence. It's not that God had gone anywhere, but Jeff's negative thoughts and desire for vengeance had moved him away from God, where love always resides. As he prayed, another Voice, one he had come to recognize as the Voice for God, the Voice for Love, urged, "Go and do your best."

Do his best? Jeff remembered a pledge of his spiritual practice: that he would seek to forgive the tiny treasons of everyday life—the rude waitress in an expensive restaurant, the employee who promised to complete a project but didn't. He knew that resisting the temptation toward revenge over smaller infractions could teach him how to handle more painful betrayals. He knew he could not lash out against every petty wrongdoing, then expect to confront a major betrayal and come out loving.

Each violation puts us at a crossroads that will forever impact our lives. Betrayal stirs strong feelings in us and compels us to take a stand.

"What stand do I take?" Jeff asked himself. "I can stand for hurt and being a martyr. Or I can stand for something greater."

〜〜〜

> "I can stand for hurt and being a martyr. Or I can stand for something greater."

〜〜〜

Finally the day of the rehearsal arrived, and he found himself climbing into the car and driving toward the church. He affirmed his faith in God, saying, "Lead me in this. All I ask is that You go before me and that I go in love. Let me go and do my best."

As he drove along, he felt the Presence of God with him, and realized God's love was bigger than his daughter's seeming betrayal. "God can see me through this," he told himself.

The gathering at the church felt awkward. Old friends, former in-laws and soon everyone would know that the real Dad was playing second fiddle to the stepfather. "Imagine what they'll think of me," he thought, and shrank with embarrassment.

Then Jeff reminded himself how much he loved his daughter and how much he loved God. "I'm here to bless her," he told himself. "And that is no small thing. This is her day, and I want to be bigger than my hurt."

During rehearsal, when the time came for Jeff to rise and do his part, the minister said to him, "I'm getting this feeling that it's going to be really awkward to have you step out of the audience to give this blessing. It would be better if before the wedding, you met me in the back room and we walk out to the pulpit together. We'll stand here for the ceremony, and then when it's time for the blessing, you'll already be here. I think I like that choreography better."

Hearing the minister's words, Jeff whispered, "Thank you, God."

The next day, as the wedding march began, the stepfather did indeed walk down the aisle with Jeff's radiant daughter. Then he sat down, the bride's back to him. But positioned next to the minister, Jeff stood face-to-face with his daughter throughout the entire ceremony. Every expression on her face became etched into his memory. And when he gave his blessing, Connie looked at him with such love and gratitude, Jeff knew he was no token in his daughter's life.

A miracle happened that day, opening the door to a rich

and rewarding relationship between father and daughter, between father and son-in-law, between grandfather and grandchildren to come. The miracle was made possible because we are created in the image and after the likeness of God, which is love. At the very core of our being, we resonate with Love's Presence, and Love expressed can transform every situation we will ever face.

Let us not open our hearts "when" and "if." Love invites us to open our hearts "in spite of." We can easily justify revenge or shrink from the world, because someone will inevitably wrong us. We can easily feel like a victim. Yet, no matter how painfully we've been wronged, in the midst of a huge temptation to be vengeful or prideful or to hold back, we have a magnificent opportunity to discover something greater. The real gift of love is that the person we think has betrayed us the most is actually an agent of the divine, offering the opportunity for grace.

~~~~~~

Let us not open our hearts "when" and "if." Love
invites us to open our hearts "in spite of."

~~~~~~

~~~~~~~~~~~~~~~~~~~~~~~~~~~~~~~~

THOUGHTS THAT TRANSFORM

~ "Getting back" at my betrayer means that I "get back" what I give. I can live a petty life or choose to live in love.

~ When I ask myself what I want most, it isn't vengeance, but love.

~ Love is more powerful than fear. Love is more powerful than retribution. Love is more powerful than hurt.

PRACTICE

Betrayal compels you to take a stand. In a moment of feeling betrayed, remind yourself, "What do I stand for? I can stand for hurt and vengeance. Or do I stand for something greater, that which gives me life. Do I stand for love?"

Recall building a mental equivalent in Chapter 6. You can utilize the same technique here. As you consider your response to the betrayal you face, how are you portrayed in the painting entitled "Revenge"? Look at the expression on your face. Notice the tension in your shoulders. Feel the tightness in your throat and the fire in your gut. Now paint a mental picture called "Love." The subject of this masterpiece has been greatly wronged but makes a stand for love nonetheless. How would you paint this individual? How does your body feel now?

Hold good thoughts. When you imagine someone who has wronged you, tell yourself, "I wish this person well." Tell yourself that even if there's no feeling behind the words, even if your last thought was that he or she should get run over by a truck. In time, the feeling will begin to follow the words. Remember, this exercise isn't about the other person. It's about bringing you to a greater, more perfect state of loving.

20. FORGIVENESS: YOU CAN'T DO IT ALONE

The situation looked hopeless. Lazarus had fallen ill and died, and his body, according to the traditions of the day, was wrapped in cloth and placed in a cave. Everybody knew Jesus healed the sick, but where was He? Many in Jerusalem quickly grew disenchanted with Jesus, because they all knew that Lazarus had been a good friend. If this "Messiah" couldn't be bothered to save a loved one, maybe He was merely a hack, a has-been miracle worker whose reputation had been vastly overrated.

"Could not this man, who opened the eyes of the blind, also have kept this man from dying?" the people of Jerusalem asked. (Many were predisposed to mistrust Jesus, as evidenced by His last visit to town, during which they tried to stone Him.)

Jesus walked twelve hours to be with His friend. He made his way through the hostile crowd into the dark cave where the body of Lazarus had already begun to decay.

There, looking at the corpse of His friend, He offered a remarkable prayer. He didn't beseech God to help Him; He didn't ask that the crowd cease their jeering. Instead, He spoke words of gratitude: "Father, I thank You that You have heard Me. And I know that You always hear Me."

Jesus knew that even in the midst of what others perceived as a hopeless situation, God would not abandon Him, God's creative energy continued to flow through Him. Jesus claimed a desired outcome in His mind. If we truly believe that faith will always lead to the manifestation of our greatest good, then gratitude is automatic. We don't have to wait until we get what we want to feel grateful. In this moment, Jesus was acknowledging that He could always count on God.

Refusing to see death in what looked like a dead body, Jesus said: "Lazarus, come forth!" and His dear friend arose.

We, too, have the capacity to call the dead back to life. We may think certain relationships have ended, but if we can move past the distance or hostility and step willingly into dark uncertainty, we have an opportunity for resurrection. "You're too late!" the villagers admonished Jesus. But He proved them wrong.

It is never too late to begin anew.

We resurrect through forgiveness. A relationship between two people may come back to life; or sometimes, a piece of ourselves may be renewed through healing. Like Jesus, we may need to travel some distance before reaching that place where we find new life. The first step toward resurrection is acknowledgment: *I have forgiveness work to do.*

~~~~~~~~

> We resurrect through forgiveness. A relationship between two people may come back to life; or sometimes, a piece of ourselves may be renewed through healing.

~~~~~~~~

There are times when I've sat with people who said, "When I ask Holy Spirit what to forgive, nothing comes up for me. There's no forgiveness work I have to do." I don't believe that's true. I do believe that we experience a level of denial about forgiveness. Maybe we don't think there's anyone to forgive because the person who wronged us doesn't deserve compassion. Holding someone beyond forgiveness takes us off the hook—or so we think. For avoiding reality doesn't change reality. Most important, denial separates us from the gift that forgiveness brings—and every one of us has a part of our mind where some resentment or hurt dwells.

A woman in our congregation received an invitation to a family reunion that she was hesitant to accept because she knew her brother would be attending. Brother and sister had not spoken in five years. When this woman spoke of their rift, her voice trembled with pain. "What should I do?" she asked me. "I could go and ignore him, just enjoy my other relatives. I could stay home. I could . . . what could I do?"

I offered her a simple five-step plan that had worked for others. It was: Get up off the couch; head to the phone; pick up the receiver; dial your brother's number; move your lips.

This plan is so simple—and carrying it out so agonizingly difficult. This woman may have every justification for shunning her brother. We have all been treated unfairly; we've all been diminished in some way or another. Who can blame us for clinging to pain? Still, hanging on takes so much effort; it saps our "aliveness," shuts us down and keeps us from experiencing the greatness of a life lived in love. Sometimes we think we're punishing a person by our refusal to communicate, but every relationship—no matter its current state—is an invitation for us to experience greater loving. Love invites us to try and bring reconciliation to anyplace where a rift exists. Understanding this, the woman in our congregation found the courage to ask, "What if I took that first step?"

Now, this woman had thought many times of calling her brother. But every time, she stopped herself in righteousness. "Look at those horrible things he said to me. He doesn't deserve my forgiveness." She never picked up the phone, but she didn't feel any better, either.

This time, she called her brother with the intent to reconcile. She did not rehash the past, because no good could come of that;

they would only start blaming one another again. She sought only to own her share of the problem.

She told him, "We haven't spoken for so long, and I'm sorry for my part in that. I hope that we can heal things between us."

She knew that her brother might reject her overture of friendliness. He might be suspicious. It's wonderful when others respond the way we want, but our reward doesn't lie in somebody else's response. Our reward comes from making a stand for love, even when our human instinct for self-protection would urge us to shut down.

As it turned out, her brother had wanted to reconcile as well, but was afraid to make the first call. The family reunion turned out to be just that. When we accept the divine invitation, there is always a celebration in store.

The first step toward resurrection is acknowledging that we have forgiveness work to do. The second step is realization: *I can't do it alone.*

I have a friend who was plagued by a problem many of us immediately relate to, and that was a bad neighbor. Somehow, we can find a way to deal with the nasty coworker or the rude salesperson, but our home is our sanctuary, and anyone who threatens the peace and security of this safe haven had better watch out.

Lisa is a single parent whose neighbors set a new standard for hatefulness. They ridiculed her religion. They screamed at her young son. They spied on her when she was tending the garden. They even parked in front of her house and posted threatening signs in the window of their truck. Once, a passerby, overhearing one of their many screaming tirades, was terrified that Lisa's life might be in danger and called 911. Another time, when a neighbor politely asked them to leave Lisa alone, they threw pots and pans at her. Lisa became ill. She began yelling back at her neighbors when they yelled at her, hating herself later for becoming the very thing that she despised.

At night, even the shadows outside her window began to feel ominous. Home wasn't supposed to be like this.

Lisa loved her neighborhood, but virtually all the other homes there were prohibitively expensive. Then, while she and her son were house-sitting (to avoid being at home), she stumbled upon her dream home, at a price she could afford.

When she hammered the "For Sale" sign into her front lawn, Lisa said to herself, "Now they'll leave me alone, because I'm going." Instead, the husband parked his monster truck in such a way that made the sign and the box of sales flyers nearly impossible for prospective buyers to see.

Lisa awakened each morning reminding herself: "I need to let this go." At the same time, such sour anger welled inside her that that every time she walked by the truck, cultured, sweet-tempered Lisa would spit on it. She fantasized that a meteor would fall on these neighbors' house. How could she possibly forgive people whose greatest joy in life was making her miserable? And should she?

The answer is that Lisa did need to forgive, not for her neighbors' sake, but her own. Lisa realized, *I can't do it alone.* How could she logically feel compassion for people whose greatest thrill in life was to make her life miserable? Logically, she could not. "I really tried," she said. "I told myself I should be grateful, because without my neighbors' harassment, never would I have found such a fabulous house.

"Then I'd take one step outside, see that hideous truck blocking my flyers and spit. Feel kindly toward these people? No way!"

Forgiveness is not intellectual. It's a shift made through Spirit. When we look at certain people, we may not see a perfect child of God, because our perception is filtered by experiences and beliefs. Hindu tradition calls this perception the veil. Every time we see a person with condemnation or judgment, the veil becomes more opaque; we see with less clarity. So we need help. We need the way God sees that person to enter into our awareness. Every time we remember love, the veil thins, and we see one another the way God intended.

〰〰〰

> Forgiveness is not intellectual.
> It's a shift made through Spirit.

〰〰〰

Eleanor Roosevelt once said, "We cause as much pain by taking offense as by giving offense." By responding spitefully to her neighbors' behavior, Lisa diminished her own aliveness. "Other people have always told me they admire how cheerful and upbeat I am, even in tough times, and that means a lot to me." Lisa wondered what these same people would find to admire in a person who walked down the street angrily expectorating on motor vehicles.

Lisa had to release her desire to punish her neighbors, as well as her nagging suspicion that this couple she found so lowly and loathsome were forcing her out. "Why are you letting them win, Mom?" her son would ask as they packed boxes.

Lisa came to recognize that inner peace meant more to her than vindication. True, she would never sit down to tea with her neighbors, but soon Lisa no longer fantasized about their untimely demise. She realized that this couple must be pretty miserable to expend so much of their energy hating. She saw that every time she had lashed back at them, she was only fueling their hatred.

By following the steps to forgiveness, Lisa began to see herself as powerful, recognizing that to stop hating required far more strength than hating. Other neighbors told her they were moved by how gracefully she handled the situation. Resenting her neighbors had sapped her energy; releasing bad feelings allowed her to devote energy instead to enjoy fixing up her dream home.

The second step to forgiveness is realization, and the third is an affirmation: *I desire a shift*. There's a difference between recognizing that we lack the power to change on our own and actually wanting to change. Do we really want to forgive? Sometimes we do not. We would rather be right, instead.

I know a man, Greg, who was devastated by his wife's infidelities. He realized that he had spent most of his adult life loving a woman he didn't even know. In an age of AIDS, hers was a dangerous lifestyle; that she would risk spreading the results of her behavior to her husband left Greg stunned. Following their divorce, he swore he'd never speak to her again.

The problem was, he could never seem to get away from her. Every woman he met was out to cheat him or cheat on him. Affection was a prelude to betrayal. Kindness was a means to manipulation. Greg rejected any woman foolish enough to get close, although few did, because they quickly tired of hearing the diatribe against his former wife.

Not until a woman stole Greg's Rolex did he change his pattern. That is, not until the so-called stolen watch surfaced under a dishcloth on the kitchen counter where he'd left it when he was chopping onions did Greg ask God for help. "I can't go on like this," he said. Greg desired a shift. He desperately wanted to be close to someone, but his venom kept him at a distance.

We think we can direct uncaring thoughts at a single person, but that negativity finds its way into all our other relationships. The places in our heart where resentment resides seep into the places we want love to live. As my minister friend Sally Rutis always says, "Holding resentment is like drinking poison and expecting the other person to die." When we seek help from God to forgive someone who has wronged us, that person doesn't suddenly become a saint. We are the ones who change.

〜〜〜

**Holding resentment is like drinking poison and
expecting the other person to die.**

〜〜〜

Through spiritual practice, Greg began to recognize the person his hatred was making him become. And he didn't like what he saw. But what could he do? He didn't want his former wife in his life. How could he cut her out and move on?

What I've learned is that relationships don't ever end. Anytime you even think of a person—difficult or otherwise—you're in relationship with that person. Greg didn't need to see his ex-wife's face to remind him of her betrayal. Relationships don't happen in a particular time and place; they occur within us.

Greg took the next step, which is a prayer: *God, help me let go.* He needed to release his anger—for his own sake—even if he and his ex-wife didn't reconcile face-to-face. There may be times for all of us that we don't heal a relationship at a human level. But we can transform it at the soul level. Jesus, the Master Teacher, said, "Go into your closet"—meaning go into your inner sanctuary, your mind, and pray there. We lift our mind to that state where we realize that Higher Power really can release for us what we never could on our own. Our Higher Power will always respond to our honest request for help.

We can sit quietly and reach out to the soul of another person, because at our very core, at a soul level, we are all pure. Our souls hold only love. Greg found himself surprisingly willing and able to take this step, because his ex wasn't present in the flesh. All the pain and personality quirks and name-calling didn't even enter into the picture. At a soul level, Greg really could wish her well.

Eventually, when he saw her in person—on the street or at family gatherings—his gut no longer lurched. They never exchanged more than a nod or a quick hello, but as Greg put it, "The difference is that as much as I once wanted her gone, mentally I made her the one controlling my life. Now, I know in some ways she'll always be there. But I'm the one who controls how I feel." In letting go of his pain, Greg found what he'd always wanted: a partner he could love and trust, first in himself, and later in a very special woman.

Do you think that God, who knows the number of hairs on your head, the number of cells in your body, and has ordered this entire universe, does not know how to heal the pain in your heart? Your willingness to release draws love to you like a magnet.

~~~~~~~

Do you think that God, who knows the number of hairs on your head, the number of cells in your body, and has ordered this entire universe, does not know how to heal the pain in your heart?

~~~~~~~

We acknowledge that we have forgiveness work to do. We recognize that it cannot be done alone. We desire to shift to a higher perspective. And when we take a step toward God and ask to let go, whatever has kept us in the shadows can no longer pose a threat. What we thought had power over us has none without our permission.

The final step is a request: *Let me forgive myself.*

Sometimes the biggest grudge we hold is against ourselves. But God holds no such grudges. Look closely at your worst moment and see if you can find some good in it.

One of the biggest mistakes I ever made was becoming pregnant my junior year in high school. That mistake hurt my parents, got me kicked out of high school and forced my boyfriend to drop out of college to marry me. That mistake shamed me deeply. I came down with a life-threatening kidney illness. Yet in the course of that illness—the night before scheduled surgery—I met a minister who introduced me to a whole new way of thinking about God, life and myself.

Without my mistake, I might never have discovered my power to cocreate with God. I might never have discovered a love so deep it would change my life. I might never have become a minister, teacher or counselor. My entire life would have been different. This tremendous shame, this seemingly unforgivable act, paved the path for a greater life than I could have ever imagined. We all make mistakes that are part of a greater design. Within each mistake lies an opportunity to learn a lesson that will bring us to a point of awakening.

Jesus probably wished that He had reached Lazarus sooner. But that didn't make Him give up. Instead, He gave thanks, knowing that even when the situation looked most hopeless, God's power was greater.

Today is a new opportunity. Remember that there is a Presence and a Power that resides in you greater than any relationship difficulty you have or have ever had. In this moment, with God, you have the opportunity to wash the slate clean and begin again. Don't keep rehearsing your mistakes and your hurts. Spirit invites you into a new beginning. It's as if God is saying: "I understand completely. Come here. Let Me put that Love around you, and be healed in it." Claim a clean slate. The Holy Spirit awaits your signal to resurrect.

Remember that there is a Presence and a Power that resides in you greater than any relationship difficulty you have or have ever had. In this moment, with God, you have the opportunity to wash the slate clean and begin again.

"What could you possibly want," *A Course in Miracles* asks, "that forgiveness does not offer?" The answer to that question is *nothing*. There is nothing more that we really want. Forgiveness offers us a way to love, it offers us a way to have deep relationships, and it offers us resurrection.

~~~~~~

THOUGHTS THAT TRANSFORM

~ Many of us think of the dark alleys of Skid Row as the epitome of an unsafe environment. But first we must look at ourselves. We must ask, "Is it safe to walk through the streets of my mind?" Jealousy, resentment and attack thoughts can turn my mind into a bad neighborhood that people shouldn't visit after dark.

~ Do I have forgiveness work to do? Let me ask myself: "Am I still breathing?" Since the answer is yes, that means I have forgiveness work to do.

~ I don't have to forgive all at once, but one hurt at a time, and I never have to do it alone.

PRACTICE

Select a relationship to resurrect.

In this relationship, you've been hurt, so acknowledge the pain. You can't heal something you can't feel.

Provide yourself incentive to follow the steps to resurrection, as outlined in this chapter. One incentive may be the gifts you receive for having let go of a grudge. Lisa, for example, earned the admiration of her neighbors and found energy to fix up her dream home. Greg found a new love. Take out a piece of paper and list five potential gifts that could arise from forgiveness. Tape this paper on your bathroom mirror or refrigerator, anyplace you are likely to see it several times a day.

Follow the steps to resurrection:

    ACKNOWLEDGE: I have forgiveness work to do.

    REALIZE: I can't do it alone.

    AFFIRM: I desire a shift.

    PRAY: God, help me let go.

    REQUEST: Let me forgive myself.

21. Teachers in Disguise

As a youngster, my daughter Jenny had a mean curveball. Every weekend, I would scream myself hoarse cheering her on at her softball games. One day, a woman toting a large garbage sack began walking through the outfield, right in the middle of the game. Her clothing appeared disheveled, her hair matted. While the players paused awkwardly, not sure how to proceed, the woman headed for the bleachers and plunked herself right down next to me.

My first thought was, "My goodness, a bag lady! Right out here in suburbia! How did that happen?"

I felt an internal nudge: *Why don't you talk to her.* My ego quickly interrupted, saying, *She doesn't look like somebody I would talk to . . . she's so . . .* In theory, I embrace all humanity equally; in reality, this woman sitting next to me smelled like sour milk, and I wanted to move as far away as possible. Maybe I could mutter something about having an errand to run and explain later to my daughter why I'd left the game before the final inning.

Explain what?

The better part of me came forward and I said, "So, how are you doing?"

She told me. Her name was Milda. She'd been living with her brother, taking care of his kids, but her brother's wife hadn't cared for Milda and three days earlier, the family had booted her out.

"Been sleeping on the streets," she said. "Don't know what I'm gonna do."

Inside me, a voice said: *Take her home.*

My intellect recoiled: *Forget that! I'm not taking this bag lady home. I mean, who is she? Maybe she's dangerous. And what about before the brother? And that odor . . .*

But the voice persisted, very calmly: *Take her home.*

I thought, *Maybe it just means take her home overnight and then figure out how we're going to help her.* Finally, as the game ended, I said, "I don't live too far from here and I know that you're hungry and you'd probably like a shower. Would you like to come home with me for a while?"

Without a word, Milda hefted her plastic bag of belongings and headed for the parking lot.

Overnight stretched into six weeks, every minute an adventure because it was immediately clear that Milda didn't know how to take care of herself very well and had some mental and emotional challenges, though none so severe that she required medicine or hospitalization.

My husband and four children were not thrilled by our new living arrangements. The kids didn't want to bathe after Milda had used the tub; my husband talked of stowing away the valuables. I awoke the first few mornings wondering, *What have I done to my family?*—then went to remove the bowls of Frosted Flakes that Milda had stashed under her bed overnight.

After those difficult first days, something about Milda began to work on us. We helped her learn how to style her hair, clean her nails and wash dishes. We savored her delight in mastering the simple routines of everyday life, routines we had always taken for granted. No, I did not let go of my intellect, which told me that it was probably not a good idea to leave Milda in charge of my children or ask her to take on a complex task. But that didn't mean I wasn't supposed to help Milda and work with her over those weeks.

We notified her brother where she was staying, and he gave Milda some news: She had received a piece of mail, an invitation to attend her thirty-year high school reunion.

"Think you could get her there?" he asked.

For the next few weeks, Milda seesawed between panic and excitement. Maybe her old classmates would laugh at her. Besides, what would she wear? I took her shopping for a new outfit. We rehearsed social niceties. And on the evening of the reunion, we sent a slightly nervous former bag lady to reminisce with the men and women who'd known the pretty, slightly shy Milda, the girl who used to help out at the cafeteria during lunch hour.

Milda came home from the reunion with a surprise: a live-in job offer. An old classmate had been looking for a caretaker for a vacation property. Milda explained that many tasks were beyond her, but she thought she could handle house-sitting. The class-mate appreciated Milda's being so honest with him about her past.

The afternoon Milda's fellow alumnus arrived, I helped her into the car and hugged her good-bye. The car pulled away from the curb, with our former houseguest waving from the passenger seat. I didn't know then that I would never see Milda again.

But just as I turned back toward my house, I heard an inner whisper: *Well done, good and faithful servant.*

I was a minister dedicated to helping others. I had performed many acts of generosity. I had striven hard to be a good wife, an exemplary mother.

Not once had I heard those words: *Well done, good and faithful servant.* No person in my past had ever challenged and stretched me to love quite the way Milda had.

I knew then that Milda had been an angel who had materialized before us in the form of a bag lady. Spirit had said, *Reach out to the one who is different. Take her home with you, because I want to get in your home and into your heart in a bigger way.* My ego would have left Milda in the bleachers. My heart reached out and learned greater love from someone I never would have suspected to be such a great teacher.

In Los Angeles, there's an interactive museum called the Museum of Tolerance. Its exhibits focus on two themes: the dynamics of racism and prejudice in America and the history of the Holocaust. The museum has two entrances, one labeled "Tolerant," the other "Intolerant." Should you try and walk through the door of tolerance, you'll find it locked, because none of us is entirely without bias. Never before had I sat next to a bag lady, and I didn't know until that moment how I would respond. Only when we acknowledge our own prejudices, those situations in which we pull back instinctively because someone is different, can we begin to move ahead.

A few years after Milda left us, my daughter Jenny was in high school and dating a young man who was African-American. Considering I'd spent my youth in peace marches and was active in the civil rights movement, I believed that I fully embraced people of all races.

Yet the strangest feeling arose in me. I asked myself, "Where did that feeling come from?" It didn't make sense. Somewhere along the line, I had been trained to believe that the color of a person's skin *did* matter. It was an old, inherited belief that was operating in me. Much as I wanted to disown the feeling, I needed to admit its presence.

Once I admitted that lurking prejudice, I asked myself if I really believed my daughter should only date or marry someone of her own race. "Ridiculous," I heard deep in my heart. The feeling I'd had was inherited "old stuff." It was not even really true for me, but it was nevertheless stored in my belief system. Once I recognized the feeling, a phantom of inherited belief, my uneasiness dissolved in the light of truth.

The Apostle Paul said, "Now we see through a glass darkly." Every one of us sees through the lens of inherited prejudices. We're seeing through the lens of distorted perceptions, judgments and criticisms that we felt at one time had some inkling of validity. Perhaps we were just too young to discern the truth.

Every one of us is a unique imprint of God's creativity. We have a God who loves differences, but a human race that struggles with them. At worst, we discriminate, sometimes in violent ways; at best we tolerate that which diverges from our set notion of what should be. How can we entertain thoughts like, "This color of skin is better than that color" or "My religion is superior to your religion" or "My sexual orientation is the only sexual orientation"? As much as we put ourselves down, we hold ourselves up as models of how people should appear, behave and believe.

Every one of us is a unique imprint of God's creativity. We have a God who loves differences, but a human race that struggles with them.

If only everyone in the world followed our example, wouldn't life be far simpler? If only our parents stopped living in the past, if only our children revered our values (and tastes!), if only our coworkers gave the same attention to detail as we do, life would be so much simpler. In my work at the United Nations, I've found that the way we deal with our most intimate relations is amplified in how nations treat one another. We all want world peace and we all want governments and countries to get along, just as we all want to feel loving toward our spouse, neighbors and children. Yet we are so quick to identify the differences we see in others as imperfections. Our human temptation is to make them wrong and ourselves right.

What Mahatma Gandhi practiced, and what Jesus embodied, is a way to deal with differences that is much greater than our present habits dictate. There's an ancient Sanskrit word, *Namasté*, that means, "The light in me recognizes and honors the light in you." Recognizing the light requires that we look beyond surface differences to the essence within. We don't better our world all at once, but we look for that light, person by person, situation by situation, peeling away one small judgment at a time. As Jesus told the multitudes, "You are the light of the world." No person was excluded.

When we seek God's guidance, we will be challenged to not only accept the differences of those around us, but to appreciate them. Mere acceptance is a kind of resignation, and there's no power in shrugging our shoulders. When we reach out to others unlike ourselves, we do not deny differences or abdicate responsibility, but open to the gifts of diversity. What grows in us is a heart that appreciates differences.

~~~~~~~~

> When we seek God's guidance, we will be challenged
> to not only accept the differences of those around us,
> but to appreciate them.

~~~~~~~~

We may never understand why a person chooses to live a certain way, but the contrast doesn't need to lead to painful condemnation. We can ask, through the power of our connection to the Divine, to accept one another as we are, and can go well beyond, to appreciate the qualities that make each of us unique.

We really can learn to recognize that something about every one of us is matchless, unrivaled. We each have a gift to give.

Try reaching out to one unlike yourself, and you will find a precious gift in the hand that reaches back.

~~~~~~

Thoughts That Transform

~ If everyone were exactly like me, life would be very dull.

~ It is only human to surround myself with people who share my interests, tastes, background and beliefs. But it is divine to reach out to the person I perceive as "different."

~ At my very core, I am a child of the same God who created every other person. God made each of us unique for a reason.

Practice

Pay attention to your heart and notice what prejudice lurks beneath the surface when you think of an individual unlike yourself, or a group of persons who seem unlike you. How can you identify that feeling as prejudice? Every person responds slightly differently—a lurch of the heart, a wrenching in the gut—but your body definitely reacts. For instance, when my daughter initially told me she was dating a young man from a different ethnic background, I had that nervous, sinking feeling I associate with standing in line for a roller coaster. (I want to be a good sport, but fast, churning rides make me seasick.) Realize where the edge of your own acceptance lies. For some people, it's around race. For others, differences in weight, intelligence, or sexual orientation cause us to pull back. We all have those boundaries, but you can't move them outward unless you know where they lie.

When you notice the familiar unpleasant feeling, instead of allowing yourself to recoil, ask your Higher Power for help in seeing this person or group from a fresh perspective. Give thanks for a chance to grow in love.

Then actively engage in making a difference. At the United Nations, I spoke about nonviolence. Just as "living the truth" extends beyond refraining from lies, "nonviolence" is bigger than the absence of destruction. Active nonviolence requires us to take a stand for something greater. For instance, in Chapter 11, "Creating Space for Grace," we met Karen, who helped turn fear about Columbine into a way for teenagers to reach out to their disenfranchised peers.

Remind yourself that God loves differences.

CELEBRATING EACH DAY

Spiritual Principle
Greatness is not found in achievement or acquisition, but in the lesson of learning to love well. Daily life is your classroom.

Once man has mastered the waves, the winds and gravity, he shall harness for God the energies of love, and then, for the second time in the history of the world, man will have discovered fire.

—Teilhard de Chardin

22. TAKE YOUR FOOT OFF THE BRAKE

It was the third day of our long-awaited vacation in Mexico, and my children and I were at a standoff. They wanted to rent four-wheelers and race through the sand dunes of Cabo, while I envisioned an afternoon lounging by the pool. Motorcycles have always struck me as great, unruly beasts I had no interest in taming.

"I'm not a motorcycle person," I explained.

"This kind has four wheels," my kids retorted.

"But it's got gears!" I prefer my vehicles to have automatic transmissions.

"You'll learn. It's easy."

Outvoted, I climbed aboard and clumsily learned to shift gears. Other than the main thoroughfare, there's hardly a paved road in Cabo, and the one we took that led out to the dunes seemed particularly plagued by potholes and other obstacles designed to make a normally upbeat woman as miserable as possible. My companions glided; I lurched. I was in the back of the line of eight four-wheelers, and my oldest son, John, kept turning around and saying, "Hurry up. You're holding up the whole group. Step on the gas."

By the time we reached the dunes, the supposed start of our journey, I was exhausted. The sand felt slippery beneath my wheels. "That was plenty for me," I said. "You guys go. I'll just wait here for you."

One by one, my grown children reiterated the teachings I had instilled in them since they were little: "Do not let fear run your life"; "Just take a baby step"; "Have faith." It was one affirmation after another until I finally relented.

Downhill was great. I coasted. But as everyone else rose gracefully on hills of sand, I dug in like a gopher. The engine roared, but I couldn't seem to move upward. It was clear that I'd been given the mutant four-wheeler, a factory reject. Nobody else got stuck. They kept yelling back at me, "Put it in third, put it in third," but I already had the thing in third gear—that much I'd figured out—to no avail. Finally my dear son-in-law, Jorge, climbed off his bike and walked over to where I sat spewing sand. So as not to embarrass me, he whispered, "Momma, you have power you are not using. Take your foot off the brake."

"Oh."

Here I was, flooring the gas pedal while keeping my foot on the brake at the same time. Of course I didn't move. The only time I'd gone anywhere was coasting downhill, which gave me the illusion of power. Coasting is motion without energy that takes you only so far. Coasting also locked up the steering mechanism, making it more difficult for me to navigate turns.

But with a single foot on the gas, I could climb any hill. I could explore, keeping up with . . . well, the next-slowest member of the group. I actually began to enjoy myself. When I allowed the vehicle to work the way it was intended to, I felt more in control than when I had unwittingly attempted to protect myself.

Ever since that vacation, my son-in-law's words have echoed in my mind. "You've got power you're not using. Take your foot off the brake." Whenever I'm attempting to accomplish something but find myself frustrated or stymied, I ask myself: "How am I holding back? Where do I have my foot on the brake?"

Unconsciously, we may have our foot on the brake right now. We may just be coasting. We have the capacity to enhance the quality of our relationships at any time, but we often find ourselves stalled, holding back from God, ourselves and others.

What makes us hold back? As children, some of us were introduced to a God that was punitive and judgmental and that only allowed a select few to get into heaven.

As adults, many of us left church, deciding that we didn't need a Higher Power. *I have enough power myself. I'll go live life on my own.* Proceeding entirely on our own will is like having one foot on the gas and the other on the brake. We cut ourselves off from the power available.

~~~~~~~~

Whenever I'm attempting to accomplish something
but find myself frustrated or stymied, I ask myself:
"How am I holding back? Where do I have my
foot on the brake?

~~~~~~~~

So what kind of God do we have? Maybe we think we have a God who is indifferent to our daily needs. Or maybe God is punitive. I think that many of us have a third idea of God as well. We may be unaware why we don't reach out. We make assumptions about God that are negative and then never look any further. We unwittingly dismiss God from our lives, much the same way we avoid a restaurant where we had a bad meal a decade earlier, a meal we can no longer even remember. We keep a distance without ever knowing the reason.

Judy, a volunteer at our church, was eighteen years old when a car accident left her paralyzed from the waist down. She spent three months in the hospital and another six months in a rehabilitation center. During that last half-year, the reality of her situation set in. She had tremendous losses to grieve. She would never again dance or hike in the woods. She had to relearn tasks most of us perform unthinkingly: getting dressed, going to the store, cooking soup.

Angry, desperately afraid of living immobilized, Judy felt punished by God. She cried for months on end. A punitive God had sought her as a target, and she didn't even know why.

She desperately wanted a new perspective, almost as much as she wanted her legs to work again. So she began trying on new ideas like clothing, looking for one that made her feel good. The idea that fit best was this: Suppose the accident was not God's punishment—just suppose God was being loving. Then what?

"I told myself, you have two options. You can cry and cry and cry and the world will support it. You certainly have something to cry about. Or, with God's help, you can do something more interesting."

Judy couldn't change her physical condition, but she had power she wasn't using. "I could take action, decide where I want to be in five years and move toward it," Judy says. "In five years, if I just let things happen, I'd get someplace, but where?"

At the time of her release from the rehabilitation center, Judy vowed not to move into a nursing home. She found a wheelchair-modified apartment and enrolled in college. There she met her future husband and earned not only a bachelor's degree in psychology, but a master's. She became a therapist to help other persons with disabilities cope with their losses. She took an active role in the community, giving speeches on increased accessibility for persons with disabilities and serving on several boards. "Just by being out there, I advocate every day," Judy says. "I drive to the grocery store, and people see I'm capable. They talk to me and want to know how the specially modified van works."

Judy is also a master bridge player and a clothing designer who describes her creations as "elegant excess." Has she stopped thinking about what it would be like to walk again? Of course not. "If offered the opportunity, I'd take it in a second," she says.

"But that doesn't make a good reason to stop living." Judy's close friends use one adjective to describe her: powerful.

We can always justify stalling. Someone or some circumstance will provide ample reason to hold back from reaching our potential. Our challenge is to harness the power within us and move ahead, even in the midst of fear or pain. When Judy stopped thinking about what she imagined God had done to her and instead recognized that she and her Creator could coauthor a rich life—a life great in love and accomplishment—her entire world shifted.

Our challenge is to harness the power within us and move ahead, even in the midst of fear or pain.

Where are you holding back right now? Do you desire to contribute to the lives of children, but don't know where to begin? Do you want a meaningful marriage but hesitate to delve into potentially troubling issues? Fear and resentment can immobilize us. Self-pity can stall us so we settle for less. Either way, we're drained of the very energy we need to accelerate the relationships we truly desire.

In a classic episode of the television show *Frasier*, the local newspaper mistakenly believes that the title character, Frasier Crane, has died and runs his obituary. Frasier, a forty-something psychiatrist who dispenses advice over the radio, is filled with regret upon seeing his entire existence boiled down to a few paragraphs of print.

"I was going to do so many things with my life," he says with a melancholy sigh. "I was going to write a novel, run for public office, do my own translation of Freud."

His producer, Roz, responds: "So what's stopping you? You're not *actually* dead."

That episode made me think about all the promises made to

ourselves that we never keep. Like Frasier, we act as if the future has already been carved into our tombstone, that it's too late to take our foot off the brake and live the way we've always intended. Through spiritual practice, we really can begin to make the difference we've always wanted. As the late comedian Joe E. Lewis said, "You only live once—but if you work it right, once is enough."

I know a woman who kept her foot pressed on the brake of her marriage, even though she wanted more than anything for her new family to succeed. Diane deeply resented her husband Jake's first wife. "I didn't marry this woman, but I'd sit down to dinner and the phone would ring. I knew that ring. It was Jane again."

Jane would phone frequently to adjust the schedule of her three-year-old son. Jake and Diane had him Saturdays, but could they take Sunday this week as well? The boy had a doctor's appointment Wednesday morning, and Jane couldn't get off work. Could Diane . . . ?

"I know my husband had no romantic interest in his former wife, but her constant presence in our lives just got me so irritated, I couldn't stand it," Diane said.

Try as she would to hide her feelings, Diane's irritation slipped through. She was sharp and curt on the phone, and the little boy could sense his stepmother's anger. He grew sullen and quiet, which upset his father. Diane found herself upset at dinner even when Jane didn't call, because she would tense up, waiting for the phone to ring.

I counseled Diane that she try asking God to help replace the irritation in her heart with a feeling of love. "When you think of this woman, you could wish her well and be glad that you can be part of helping her succeed."

Diane's response was "I want my marriage to work, but I don't care if she does well or not."

Her feeling was part of her human nature. But remember, we have a divine side as well. In First John, we read, "God is love." As children of our Creator, we, too, are beings of love. Resentment violates our divine nature, causing us to expend more energy in resenting other people than in being loving. It causes us to focus our energy on limitation rather than love. It fuels our sense that the world and the people in it are against us, and puts the brakes on our ability to experience the good that is here. We find our way back to love by practicing perfect loving in imperfect relationships.

"Okay," I told her. "Just try saying these words to yourself: "Jane, I wish you well"—even if you don't mean them. You don't have to be a saint. You don't have to be perfect. But my guess is that there's more love in your heart than you're showing.

"Aren't you even a little bit curious what would happen if you let just a little more out?"

This was a radical idea for Diane. She believed that all her love should be expended on her husband and stepson, because those were the people who mattered. To practice loving an irritant didn't sit well with Diane, but she was willing to consider that there might be a better way. She knew that her resentment of Jane was so strong it could never vanish on its own, so she began by telling God: "I'm willing to be willing to feel differently."

Notice she didn't say, "I'm willing to love Jane." That would have been too great a step for her to take. Yet, begrudgingly at first, she decided to send Jane five good thoughts a day, even though the feeling behind them wasn't present yet. "I really do wish you well"; "I hope you're happy"; "I hope that you really do get that new job that you want."

Weeks passed. As she continued her practice of good thoughts, Diane began to notice that Jane's calls bothered her less. She wasn't overjoyed to hear that familiar voice, but she wasn't upset, either. "Maybe this is working," she thought.

As more time passed, she came to know and appreciate Jane as a person. Diane hadn't understood the reality of single parenthood and saw that the woman she'd labeled demanding and disorganized had actually been frightened. The good thoughts Diane had once sent skeptically now felt genuine.

As a result, Jane doesn't always have to call to work out her son's schedule—Diane might call first instead. The two women attend the boy's school performances together, for Diane genuinely wishes Jane well. Diane's stepson has relaxed, and so has Jake, who had felt torn between his wife and the mother of his son. Diane, in learning an unbridled love, received the greatest blessing of all. She is much happier, and her relationship with her family has blossomed.

"By holding back compassion from Jane, I was holding back my marriage, and I didn't even know it," Diane told me later. "I didn't know it was possible to feel this great.

"But I think God knew all along."

Thoughts That Transform

~ God's power in my life is limited only by my unwillingness to receive it.

~ Resentment dissolves in the presence of love.

~ To brake is human, to release divine.

Practice

Take out a sheet of paper and draw a line down the middle. On the left side, write: "What I Think God Is." Your God may punish or condemn. Your God may only accept others who are holier than you. Maybe yours is a God of desperation, to be called on a 911-to-heaven line reserved only for emergencies.

On the right side of the paper, write: "What I Want God to Be." When I did this practice, I wrote that I wanted God to be all-loving and all-powerful. I wanted God to be all-forgiving and to offer assurance that I am forgiven. I wanted God as my constant companion, ensuring my safety and comfort. I wanted God to guide me to wisdom, creativity and beauty and to nudge me in the right direction when I forget all that I want to be. I wanted God to be all this and more for me and for everyone.

Finished? Tear your paper in half and throw the left side away. What remains is your new concept of God, a God who is loving, giving, all-powerful and always present. Every time you remind yourself of this larger, more loving concept of God, you take your foot off the brake.

23. WHY POSTPONE HAPPINESS?

While shopping one day for new clothes, Gail happened across the perfect wedding gown. It was creamy satin, with elaborate beading and a scalloped hem. The sleeves billowed romantically, suggesting the designer's fondness for Victorian novels, and best of all, the price was right. Gail, then thirty-seven and recently returned to her hometown of Portland for a job with an established law firm, tried on the dress and pronounced it perfect. Staring at her reflection in the mirror, Gail could imagine herself walking slowly down the aisle, all eyes on the radiant bride in her beaded splendor. She took her newly purchased gown to her newly rented apartment and hung it in the bedroom, behind her wool suits, where it remained for two weeks, until Gail could bear its presence no longer.

There in her closet, the frock mocked her. It was not Gail's style—not even close. Away from the muted lighting in the boutique, the dress revealed itself as borderline cheap: slightly gaudy, the satin too shiny, the sleeves cartoonish in their fullness.

"My Lord, what was I thinking?" Gail asked herself.

"Maybe a high school sophomore could wear it to a prom, but a thirty-seven-year-old woman should definitely not wear this when she gets married," Gail told herself.

And therein lay the greater source of her embarrassment: No wedding date had been set. Known for her no-nonsense approach in court, Gail had behaved in a manner seemingly at odds with her unerring practicality on the job: She had spent money on an article of clothing despite evidence contradicting the necessity of it. The truth of the matter was that at the time she bought the dress, Gail very much wanted to be married, but she was not engaged to anyone. She wasn't even dating.

"I told myself I was practicing creative visualization," Gail recalls. "This was my visual road map. This was my dream. This little icon in front of me would then manifest with clear intention." Only the process had made her feel worse, not better, and the offending gown went back to the store. At least, Gail could console herself, "I haven't picked out a china pattern."

Like many single women, Gail had watched, smiling and congratulatory, as one by one her friends had proceeded down the aisle and advanced directly into motherhood, and she was sick of the endless processional. "It really got redundant," she says. By contrast, "long-term relationships" for her meant three months, and those were the good ones. It was not that she begrudged her friends their happiness (not most of the time, anyway); she simply wanted her fair share, and their joy underscored her own frustration. Her marital status stuck out like a naked ring finger.

Gail felt lonely. Not only was she without a husband, she felt abandoned by her friends. These women with whom she had once exchanged confidences about the angst of relationships now looked at her, as she tried to articulate her pain, quite uncomprehendingly, as if marriage had induced selective amnesia. They just didn't get it.

"Don't worry, you're so pretty, so smart, your time will

come," everyone told her, to which she responded, "Thank you," smiling politely, but secretly seething inside: "Then why the hell hasn't it happened, and why don't you introduce me to somebody?"

~~~~~~

The pang of aloneness is almost indescribable to those who've forgotten how it feels, just like a full stomach erases the taste of hunger.

~~~~~~

So full were her friends' lives with Pampers and wallpaper patterns, they no longer remembered what it felt like to be alone. Worse yet, these women, as far as Gail could see, hadn't done anything to merit their easy good fortune, while she, on the other hand, had diligently embarked on a spiritual path. She prayed. She tithed. She forgave. And she would see her friends who "weren't aware, weren't awake, weren't even conscious, and they kept getting married and having babies," Gail says.

Gail's divorce at age thirty-one had led to her spiritual awakening. "I got very clear about what I wanted," she says. "I wanted to be happily married. I still had ovaries willing to function, and I wanted a child.

"I knew there would be a time of healing and course-correcting after my divorce. I thought it would maybe take something like six months."

The years passed, but Gail remained alone. Every night after work, she would note the "For Sale" signs on houses on her way home, thinking, "How I'd love to own that bungalow! What I couldn't do to fix up that Cape Cod!" But "No," she told herself, "I can't buy a house. Not by myself. It's too lonely. I'll wait a little longer until . . ."

So Gail remained alone in her apartment. Her pain peaked one day when a former roommate left a message on her answering machine saying, "Gail, give me a call. I've got some exciting news!" Great—another bridal shower to organize. Gail was happy for her friend, but the part she calls her "small self" could not help but feel wronged. This woman, not the easiest person to get along with and lacking in spirituality to boot, had cruised effortlessly into marriage while Gail spent weekends alone.

She wrote in her journal, "Dear God, I am so angry at you. How could you forsake me? Why doesn't this ever happen for me?"

Every now and then, she would hear a Voice within her respond: "Fear not." Gail tried to be unafraid of being alone, but it didn't work. She'd focus momentarily on all the good things in her life and then, as she put it, "get stuck in my own mud."

Many of us deeply yearn for what Gail wanted: the fulfillment of a loving relationship. The pang of aloneness is almost indescribable to those who've forgotten how it feels, just like a full stomach erases the taste of hunger. When the promotion comes, and there's no one with whom to celebrate, when the disposal conks out and the only person to plunge her hand down the drain is you—in moments large and small, the missing partner's presence looms. Friends who hadn't walked in Gail's shoes advised, "Look, you've got so much going for you. Why don't you focus on the good stuff instead of looking for a man?"

But Gail's focus on what was missing made sense to her. As we've seen, our tendency is to follow the path of human nature, which frequently and logically leads us to do the very thing that makes us feel the worst. It made perfect sense to Gail that being alone should overshadow everything else. She didn't have to take a college course on "Saving Love for a Life You're Not Living"; she didn't check out "Fifteen Ways to Postpone Happiness" from the library. No, she followed the well-trod path of human nature, acutely aware of traveling solo.

Eventually, Gail tired of the journey. She wondered if there might be a new direction for her to take, one that did not leave her feeling so sad and alone. "Fear not," she heard once more, and very tentatively, she began to change direction. The Divine side of her knew that she could have a very real companion in God, but the human side was in such pain, Gail had a hard time feeling anything beyond her own loneliness. "I'd worked so hard on my spirituality, but God always felt so far away," Gail says. "Now I tried to imagine that God was with me, all the time." With God as her companion, Gail still longed for a strong human relationship. But no longer did she feel so overwhelmingly alone.

~~~~~~

With God as her companion, Gail still longed for a strong human relationship. But no longer did she feel so overwhelmingly alone.

~~~~~~

"I felt like I had screwed up my life. I was married in my twenties when I should have been single, and single in my thirties when I should have been married. All my hope for marriage and a happy life was disappearing and dissipating. I had resolved that my time might not come, but that if I could never have a child, I could at least be 'good Auntie Gail.' "

She resolved to awaken every morning thanking God for each day and vowing to remember Him throughout the day. As she began to feel the Presence more profoundly, she felt guided to try something new.

"I want a house, a garden and a dog," Gail repeated to herself, and those three desires repeated themselves in her mind like a mantra. Ideally, her house would have a husband in it as well, but she asked herself why she should deny herself one thing because she couldn't have another. "I'm not going to put my life on hold a moment longer," she declared, and bought a bungalow with a small garden. The dog was another matter.

" 'I want a house, a garden and a dog.' That was God telling me, 'These are the steps you can take alone.' I undertook two of the steps, but I never gave myself permission to have it all," she says. For the dog symbolized something more than furry companionship—a dog meant that she had given up the hope of romantic love. At age thirty-nine, Gail felt her biological clock ticking like a time bomb. As a pet owner, she reasoned, she would need to head right home each evening after work, which would leave her unavailable for cocktail dates, one of which could lead to a serious relationship, which in turn might lead. . . . Quite simply, she didn't want Fido wreaking havoc on her matrimonial plans.

Two years after the ill-fated wedding dress venture, something in Gail let go.

"I had prayed so fervently, and what I wanted hadn't happened, that I thought, 'Maybe I'm not listening. Maybe God has another plan for me. Maybe the glory of my life will look different from what I'm willing to consider.' "

It's in the midst of the pain—those times when the tendency is to hold back—that we have the greatest opportunity for perfect loving.

Gail knew she could choose to have love in her own house every time she unlocked the door. While she was attending a retreat put on by our church, a thought rushed into her mind. "You're still withholding from yourself. If you want a dog, go get one. Celebrate your life NOW!" As she said these words, the weight of her loneliness lifted. In a moment of clarity, she realized she was no longer just mouthing the words, "Thank you, God, for this day," but feeling truly grateful. She could live in the love God offered. And God's love was certainly something to celebrate.

During the retreat, Gail got to know a volunteer from the church, David, a sales executive. The two exchanged phone numbers and he invited her hiking. In turn, Gail invited David to accompany her dog-hunting. There, at the Humane Society, she knew instinctively that the English setter-Brittany spaniel mix wagging its tail at her was destined to go home with her. Molly and Gail became best friends, and the love that had so long been denied her came rushing to greet her, tail wagging, each evening when she opened the door. "To this day, I look at her and believe she is my gift from God," Gail says. At the same time, her relationship with David, whom Gail had at first considered a casual friend rather than a potential mate, developed into something more.

Gail celebrated her fortieth birthday in Greece, on her honeymoon with David. And she hasn't stopped celebrating.

This story could easily have had a different ending. Gail might not have found her soul mate. She might still be the one who doesn't catch the bouquet. Would she still be celebrating? Or would she have given up on love?

As Gail is the first to point out, her newfound attitude is precisely what allowed someone else to love her. Had she not shifted from "Gotta get a man" to "I have so much to enjoy today," David might have been "scared off at once," she says. A desperate determination to marry is about as inconspicuous as that first wedding gown Gail selected. She also appeared more balanced. When Gail met David, she didn't pour out all her stored-up love on him, which can frighten off any potential partner. Gail had already taken that stored-up love and spread it around, on her home, her dog and a new group of friends.

If she and David had never met, and Gail had remained without a partner, I know that she would undoubtedly have experienced moments of great loneliness. But I also know that she would no longer have felt alone. Gail would not have given up on love so much as she'd have relinquished her inflexibility about what it means to love and be loved.

It's in the midst of the pain—those times when the tendency is to hold back—that we have the greatest opportunity for perfect loving. When we participate in our own miracles, the windows of heaven open and fill us with divine strength. Dare to love life now. After all, what are you waiting for?

Thoughts That Transform

~ If I make a commitment to loving, that is far greater than committing to love a particular individual.

~ Every person I encounter, every relationship I touch, is enriched if I choose to be loving.

~ I celebrate today.

Practice

Has anyone ever asked you, "So what did you do this last weekend?" or even "What did you do yesterday?" only to have you respond with a blank stare, unable to conjure up a single event from the past twenty-four hours? Obviously, you were busy, perhaps even efficient, but nothing about that period of time was sufficiently meaningful to create a memory. Think of what things you might do this very day to bring you joy. Then proceed.

Identify an area where you are postponing happiness.
Waiting for a man, Gail denied herself a home, a dog and a
garden. I know a single dad who relished the idea of a special
dinnertime with his children. But by the time he got home from
work, he was always too exhausted to create an elaborate meal.
So he would plunk down microwaved macaroni and cheese—
whatever was handy—and the kids would dine in the den with
Home Improvement *reruns. Cooking a nice meal took on*
ominous proportions, like preparing a banquet. Then the dad
realized he was postponing more than a good meal. "Why
can't we all sit at the dining table, eat off the good china and
light candles, even if we've got McDonald's?" he asked
himself. "This could be a special time, but it can't be special if
it never happens." What special time could you be celebrating
right now?

24. CLAIMING YOUR GREATNESS

When Jesus was thirty years old, He and His mother attended a wedding reception at which the host committed the ultimate social gaffe: running out of wine. Libations were hardly a guest's responsibility, so Jesus may have been a bit nonplussed when Mary said to Him, rather pointedly: "They have no more wine."

Obviously, Mary didn't expect her son to dash out to the Galilee minimart for a case of Chablis. She was challenging Him to perform some miracle that would save the party.

When we remember the spectacular greatness of Jesus—healing the sick, walking on water, even resurrecting the dead—it's easy to forget that His powers emerged gradually. At this point, He didn't have a single miracle to His credit, and even playing vintner to thirsty guests must have seemed beyond His capacity.

Thus Jesus responded as would any adult male anxious to get Mom off his back: "Woman, what does your concern have to do with Me? My hour has not yet come."

When opportunity arises to call forth the greatness within ourselves—to embark on or deepen a relationship, to express the feeling in our heart, to make a difference in the world—there's a tendency to say, "Who, me? I'm not ready for that." Or as Jesus put it: "My hour has not yet come."

The ever-wise Mary dismissed her son's qualms, command-ing the servants, "Whatever He says to you, do it."

At that very moment, Jesus began to fulfill His destiny. In-stead of turning away from what seemed an impossible task, He initiated a spiritual practice we can call "acting as if." Behave as if the miracle you desire is already a reality. Seeing six stone wa-ter pots, Jesus told the servants to fill the jugs with water and carry them to the bride's father.

As he sipped the liquid, it transformed from water into wine, and he pronounced that the best vintage had been "saved for last." The festivities continued without further interruption.

Acting as if puts our belief into action. The trouble is, we often act as if we believe in nothing greater than our present circumstance. If we believe in the problem at hand more than we believe in God, relationships stagnate; they never grow be-yond our limited thinking. We *act as if* a demanding job, unpaid bills, a child home sick with the flu are good reasons to put off developing great relationships. Sorry, but life never pauses that long.

Waiting until the "right time" to focus on relationships is like telling ourselves, "I'm too busy to breathe today. And the next few days are packed. But next Tuesday, I'll really take in some good oxygen." Relationships are as full as the life we breathe into them.

As we've seen, one powerful way to transform a relationship is to lay hold of our desire—greater intimacy with a child or partner, parent or friend—and to vividly picture the result. Ask: "What would a great relationship with my spouse, partner, child or friend look like, and how would it feel?"

Now we're ready to take action. *Act as if* this great relation-ship already exists. In Mark 11:24, we read: "Therefore I say to you, whatever things you ask believe that you have received them and you will receive them." This is the entrance to the realm of infinite possibility. When we act as if nothing can stop us from fully loving, we start loving more fully.

I once read a newspaper article about another miraculous wedding feast. A woman and her fiancé had planned a lavish, $13,000 wedding reception at a Boston hotel. The day the invitations were mailed, the groom-to-be backed out, and the spurned bride, after contacting her guests, went to the hotel to retrieve her 50 percent deposit. While the manager commiserated with her, he stuck to the hotel policy: The bride could only get a $1,300 refund. Having been homeless ten years earlier, she was loath to waste money. She could feel sorry for herself or she could celebrate her good new beginning as a woman who was healthy, financially secure and free of a man who was obviously lousy husband material for her. Why slink away in shame? she told herself. Acting as if she had great cause to celebrate, she did just that. The jilted bride threw a party, after all—not a wedding banquet, but a big blowout.

After changing the main course to boneless chicken—in honor of the groom—she sent invitations to rescue missions and homeless shelters, spending her nest egg treating the down-and-out of Boston to a night on the town. So one warm summer evening, people accustomed to peeling half-gnawed pizza off cardboard dined instead on chicken cordon bleu. Hyatt waiters in tuxedos served hors d'oeuvres to senior citizens propped up by crutches and aluminum walkers; bag ladies, vagrants and addicts took one night off from the hard life on the sidewalks and feasted on chocolate wedding cake. Everyone danced to big-band melodies late into the night. The nonbride went home that night with a partner who would never jilt her—herself, as she discovered that she had the inner resources to face whatever difficulty came her way.

I know many people who found a miracle in misfortune by *acting as if*. A television producer laid off from work during a period of downsizing at first felt resentful, because others with less seniority had not been let go. Then he decided to *act as if* a greater job awaited. Thanking God for this unexpected opportunity, he interviewed with confidence, never once maligning his former employer. At one point, he had thought the producer job the pinnacle of his career; but his next job was so much better, he realized that, as with the wine, the best had been saved for last.

When my mother, a former executive, felt somewhat lost after retirement, she created a support group for other retirees who were wondering how they might spend the rest of their lives. She called the group New Horizons to remind people that sometimes life saves the best for last. Over the last dozen years, I have heard story after story from Mom about how Faye or Walt or Marie began to *act as if* and ended up embarking on a whole new adventure in living.

You are invited to the wedding feast not just once, but every day. The wedding feast is your life. Your potential to create great relationships remains water until you *act as if* and draw it out; only then does it become wine.

~~~~~~~~~

> You are invited to the wedding feast not just once,
> but every day. The wedding feast is your life. Your
> potential to create great relationships remains
> water until you *act as if* and draw it out; only
> then does it become wine.

~~~~~~~~~

Most of us hesitate to take this step. Indeed, spurned brides throwing themselves a reception are sufficiently rare that a newspaper sent a feature writer to the Boston bash.

We can learn to *act as if* in stages. First, the television producer, the retiree and the bride-not-to-be committed to holding a particular worldview. They would not have risked venturing into the unknown unless they believed that life was benevolent. Jesus held the same worldview. Having never made wine before, He didn't know that He had the ability, but He proceeded as if it were possible that something absolutely intoxicating could emerge from a substance as ordinary as water. Ask yourself: "Is the life I believe in malevolent or benevolent?" All relationships are predicated on the answer to this question.

Most people are happy when things go well and sad when plans or hopes go awry, and are disconnected from the dynamic power within to choose how they respond. Generally, we spend far more energy trying to prevent bad things from happening than we do challenging our notions of what could be.

Do you have a tendency to see the good in people and situations? I know some people whose childhoods were difficult who are so filled with bitterness toward their parents they believe nothing good can ever happen for them, and from this perspective, that prophecy continues to be fulfilled. I know others whose early years were equally painful and say that as a result, they have a deeper desire to assist others in pain, a deeper appreciation for the loved ones in their life.

I once saw a bumper sticker that read: "We come into the world naked, wet and hungry, and it goes downhill from there." If that's the world we believe in, we will find injustice and oppression at every turn. Other people rarely have our best interest at heart. Simple kindness is suspect and cruelty serves to validate our negative perceptions. We lean toward negativity and pessimism, taking a certain sour satisfaction whenever our belief is proved right. Clichés spout from our lips: "You can't fight city hall" or "The rich get richer and the poor get poorer." The more we move toward the malevolent worldview, the less inclined we are to act as if, because sticking our neck out means that someone will cut it off. How can we possibly experience great relationships in a world conspiring against us?

Now imagine someone who inhabited a world of evil beyond

what even the worst pessimist could imagine—and still made a choice for good. One of the people who has had the most profound impact on my worldview is the psychologist Victor Frankl. Interned in a Nazi concentration camp during World War II, he watched as, one by one, all the people he loved were put to death. His own life was spared, but he was forced to stand naked in front of a German tribunal that burned his life's work. As a final humiliation, one of the guards demanded he relinquish his wedding ring. The anguish of that moment, the culmination of all he had lost, was almost too much for one soul to bear. There was nothing left.

Yet, as he reached for that band—the last vestige of his former life—something shifted inside him.

In a flash, Frankl realized he had not lost everything. He saw that there exists a single God-given freedom that no one can steal without permission, and that is the freedom to respond. He chose a response that defied the carnage, the unspeakable inhumanity that filled his every waking hour.

The Nazis thought they had stripped him of every semblance of power, leaving a helpless, hate-filled victim. But they were wrong.

"You cannot make me hate," Frankl decided.

There exists a single God-given freedom that no one can steal without permission, and that is the freedom to respond.

That refusal to hate in the face of overwhelming hatred allowed him to see courageous expressions of love in the direst conditions. He saw great love expressed between prisoners, such as one offering another a portion of his meager meal. He even noticed traits and characteristics he could admire in some of the guards.

Frankl's belief that it was not the situation but our response that matters formed the foundation for his entire body of work, books and stories that would touch millions of people in the years to come.

We do not create every circumstance we experience, but we do create our experience of every circumstance we are in. We all have a response-ability. The ability to respond however we choose, regardless of our loss, is God's gift to us.

A benevolent worldview enables us to risk *acting as if*. If we want relationships to flourish, we imagine them already in bloom. We act confidently, versus spending our energy fretting over what might go wrong. There's a story about a little boy who went to a town meeting where the farmers were terrified about a drought. The minister called the farmers together to pray and asked them to bring symbols of their faith. People brought crosses and prayer books and Bibles and prayed and prayed and prayed. Nothing happened, but then the little boy arrived, and the heavens opened up with a torrent of rain. And then they saw his symbol of faith: He had brought an umbrella.

What would "bringing an umbrella" look like in a relationship?

If one of our adult children doesn't call for several weeks, a malevolent worldview would lead us to think: "He doesn't really appreciate everything I've done for him over the years, or he wouldn't neglect to call me." Or, "All he ever wants is money or a favor." Or, "I guess I'm just some throwaway mom."

Should we take an umbrella to the relationship, however are showing that we believe in our closeness more than distance, that we believe in love more than fear. That w causes us to act as if nothing can keep us apart. "Gos' spoken with my son in so long. My fingers can dia' well as his. He must have a lot going on right r tell him how much I believe in and love him. Or I of him as a little boy, put it in a card and send it to him with a note telling him how proud I am that this precious child grew into the man he has become."

If we believe it's going to rain, then we walk and act differently even in the midst of a drought.

~~~~~~~~

If we believe it's going to rain, then we walk and act differently even in the midst of a drought.

~~~~~~~~

After the breakup of a long-term relationship, a friend of mine, fed up with her depression, decided to act as if she was joyful, confident and full of hope for the future. "But giving myself these positive messages didn't work," Sharon told me. "I'm a person of action, so I created a very simple action plan. I vowed, no matter what, to do one new thing a day."

Sharon would never have pushed herself this way unless she believed good would come, and it did.

She started small. She shopped in a new grocery store. She and her son ate dinner in a new restaurant. She sat down with a cup of coffee at an unfamiliar coffee shop. She said hello to people at work she'd never met. By opening herself to a new circle of people—acting as if only good could come—Sharon found that others responded positively to her. And she began to feel a measure of the confidence she'd been seeking. "I began expanding the idea of one new thing a day to doing things in a way I normally wouldn't before." For instance, she ran into an old acquaintance at the movies. "Give me a call sometime," the woman said. The old Sharon would always let the other person initiate the call. This time, however, she decided, "I will call." A casual acquaintance turned into a close friend.

A good friend of Sharon's told her he felt bad about her d romance and asked if there was anything he could do to help. Normally, Sharon would have said, "Of course not. I'm just fine," all the while thinking, "I'm forty years old and while everybody else in the world is married, I'm all alone."

In keeping with her practice of "one new thing a day," Sharon told John: "You know, I really am feeling much better, but what I want in life is a fulfilling romantic relationship. Do you have any great single friends for me?"

John did not. But so moved was he that the normally stoic Sharon chose to confide in him, John tried something new himself: Without telling Sharon, he embarked on a mission to find his friend the perfect mate, calling around to inquire about kind, sensitive, eligible males. The sixth call paid off. Mission accomplished, John told Sharon what he'd done and asked permission to give out her phone number.

After her initial mortification passed ("Thank God he didn't use my name when calling everyone he knew!"), Sharon felt flattered John had gone to such trouble. The blind date sounded extremely intriguing. She hoped her phone would ring soon.

Only, it did not. Weeks passed without a word from the potential Mr. Wonderful. "Great," Sharon thought, "I've been rejected before the first date. Even for me, that's a record." The old Sharon would have thrown herself a pity party. "But I'm acting as if the world wants to do me good. I'm acting as if I really can have fulfilling relationships."

Sharon mustered her courage to do one new thing that would have been unimaginable before. Calling John, she said, "You know, I never heard from that fellow. Maybe it's not meant to be, but . . . maybe he got my number wrong. Why don't you try again." John immediately called his friend, who called *his* friend, who, sure enough, had reversed two digits of Sharon's number. When the two finally did get together, Sharon said, she felt as if she had stepped right into a fairy tale.

Unlike its counterpart in fairy tales, however, the magic in this story wasn't in a potion or wand. It resided in Sharon, who dared enough to act as if she was destined for great relationships.

~~~~~~

THOUGHTS THAT TRANSFORM

~ While some grief and loss are inevitable in my lifetime, suffering is optional.

~ No matter what is happening in my life, I can choose to respond in joy.

~ My relationships are as full as the joy I breathe into them.

~ When I *act as if*, the *if* becomes my reality.

PRACTICE

Recognize how your current worldview influences every aspect of your life.

Carefully cultivate a more positive viewpoint. Take any situation in a relationship—such as the one I used about an adult child's failing to call—and list three things that a malevolent worldview would lead you to think. Then list three beliefs that would arise from a benevolent worldview.

What action might a benevolent worldview prompt you to take? (Remember that life will graciously support whatever view you adopt.)

Take the step. "Act as if" your positive worldview reflected reality.

To fortify your worldview and enable you to "act as if" more readily, experiment with trying one new thing a day. This is a spiritual stretch. You're reaching beyond what you know, trusting that your risk will lead to good. Start small. Take a different route home from work. Shop at a new grocery store. Vary your workout routine. I realize those steps may not sound terribly spiritual, but you're conditioning yourself to stretch a bit further. If you're lonely, consider something as simple as saying hello to three new people a day. If your child seems distant, act as if you were close and invite your child on a special outing, just the two of you. Invite an estranged friend or relative to dinner.

25. RITUALS OF LOVE

A friend once confided to me that she yearned for the kind of relationship with her husband she had when they first met, when getting to know one another filled their lives with excitement, mystery and wonder. "I liked the silly poems Charlie used to leave me on the windshield of my car," she said. "Now the only notes I get from him are a reminder to pick up his suit at the dry cleaner's. Wouldn't it be great if we could go back to the beginning again?"

Not necessarily. What I've found is that while the novelty of that initial surge of romance keeps us euphoric for a time, the exchanges that develop between two people who know one another well can be far more meaningful. Earlier, we talked about how our natural curiosity can continue to fuel the thought and thoughtfulness that characterize the early phase of a relationship. Loving rituals are another way to practice perfect loving.

Rituals are activities we do repeatedly that demonstrate to a loved one: "My relationship with you matters to me. I commit to investing the energy, time and devotion to make sure you know and feel that."

Most of us reserve rituals for holidays or birthdays. We serve special foods, haul out the good china. The very smell of roasting turkey evokes memories of Thanksgivings past, filling us with a sense of security and connection with family. But we don't have to wait for a certain date on the calendar to perform a loving ritual. We can incorporate rites of loving into our daily life.

~~~~~~

We don't have to wait for a certain date on the calendar to perform a loving ritual. We can incorporate rites of loving into our daily life.

~~~~~~

We begin with a question: "What can I do today—for my partner, parent, friend or child—that demonstrates how much that person matters to me?"

Often, we tend to give love only in the way we want to receive it. Yet those close to us have preferences different from our own. Some respond best to written words. Others prefer touch. Some love a demonstration of beauty, such as a bouquet of flowers. What makes establishing rituals so exciting is that we have the opportunity to discover that mysterious part of a loved one and to demonstrate how special that person is to us.

A man I know, Peter, travels frequently on business. Ever since his mother had moved to an assisted living facility, he'd brought her a present from each trip, such as perfume from France, a silk scarf from Thailand, crystal from Austria. Then one day he went to retrieve his mother's coat from her closet, and *thunk!*—the crystal vase fell right on his head. Investigating further, Peter discovered an entire stash of his luxury items, many still in their original box. At first, Peter was hurt. He'd gone to a great deal of trouble to select presents representative of the countries and cities he'd visited.

"Honey," his mother said, "I appreciate your generosity. When I had the house, it was different. But take a look around. I'm in this tiny place. I don't have much use or space for more 'stuff.' "

"Isn't there anything I've brought that you like?"

"Well . . . those Swiss chocolates were out of this world. It was a real treat for me to be able to share them with the other residents."

The proverbial lightbulb went off in Peter's bruised head. His mother had always adored chocolate, but even more, she had always relished playing hostess. "Mom must really miss not being able to entertain anymore," he thought.

From then on, Peter never failed to bring his mother a huge box of specialty chocolates from his trips. This ritual gave birth to another custom: Upon receiving her gift, Peter's mother would invite the other residents over to sample the truffles, mints and cremes, the gracious hostess once more. The custom brought her great joy, continuing even after she became bedridden.

A truly loving ritual can endure indefinitely. From the time he could form sentences, my youngest son, Mat, liked to have his back rubbed when he awakened in the morning. Now, when he's home on a break from college and I go to wake him up, he smiles at me as I remember this predilection and once again rub his back.

Coffee enters into some of my own preferred rituals. Thirty years ago, when I met my then next-door neighbor Colleen, she and I began drinking coffee together and started a ritual of buying one another a mug each year. For the next year, we would drink out of those mugs, each of us saying a brief prayer for the other as we sipped our morning coffee. The following year, we would buy new mugs for each other at Christmas. At one point, we lived two thousand miles apart, but the ritual kept us thinking of one another every day.

Every Sunday morning, I meet four senior managers at our church at six o'clock, before services. There's an all-night Starbucks a few miles from my house, and one morning, I surprised the managers with their favorite coffee drinks. I saw how much they appreciated the gesture, and now it's become a regular Sunday activity of mine. Playing the Sunday coffee lady has become a ritual that says, "I'm thinking of you. I appreciate all that you do."

I know a single mother who says "I love you" with tea. "Whenever we decide to celebrate something, I throw a tea party for my daughters," Karen says. To commemorate the first snowfall of the year, Karen and her girls dressed all in white for a party in which meringues and Russian tea cakes were served. When Karen's second daughter was born, she put on a party for her older girl, decorating cupcakes with baby paraphernalia. At the Christmas tea, everyone makes ornaments and wrapping paper. A visit from a close friend may inspire a tea party. "Or sometimes, we just have tea to celebrate being together," Karen says. Her oldest daughter enjoys the ritual because it makes her feel sophisticated, transporting her to a different time and place. Interestingly, when the girls were little, they could stomach the tea only if it was drowned in cream and sugar. "It wasn't about the *tea*," Karen explains. "It makes the girls feel special and differentiates the moment, creating a memory."

Karen—a self-described queen of ritual—developed a wonderful custom to cap off summer that she calls Kids in Charge. Armed with maps of Oregon and highlighting pens, the girls plan a road trip, with every detail left to their devices, from what to pack to whether or not the pets get to come along. The girls agree on a particular destination or decide to end up wherever life takes them. They have goals for each trip—once, it was to milk a cow—and are encouraged to think through their choices. For instance, when "eating nothing but cookies all day" was proposed, Karen pointed out that stomachaches might be in the offing, but it was still their choice. The family looks forward to the trip every summer, which also serves to ease everyone's way back into the school year.

Loving rituals can be a holiday of our own making or a simple, everyday gesture, such as putting a bath towel out for your partner. Each morning, Ed or I, whoever showers first, leaves a clean towel for the other, so the first thing we receive to start the day is an "I care about you" message. Over the years, I have purchased fluffy new towels and had them monogrammed with loving sayings such as "Man of My Dreams," then left them over the shower stall to greet my husband when he awakens.

~~~~~~~~

Loving rituals can be a holiday of our own making or a simple, everyday gesture.

~~~~~~~~

Every Sunday, I give Ed a card. He not only cherishes the words, but appreciates how much energy I devote each week to looking for just the right sentiment. Every Tuesday, Ed presents me with a gorgeous bouquet. I adore the flowers and the card he includes, but knowing that he is consciously thinking "I want to show Mary how much I care" is the real gift.

One time, Ed altered his floral ritual to celebrate my arrival home from India. Having spent the last fifty hours on planes, trains and buses, I nearly collapsed when Ed greeted me at the airport gate with a cup of my favorite coffee. Upon reaching the car, he pulled out a bouquet of roses. Then he opened the passenger door. I was dumbfounded. Rose petals covered every inch of the car seat and the floor beneath it. Ed bent down, slipped off my shoes and placed my feet in the petals.

Those rose petals were exquisite. Yet my husband's thoughtfulness was even more so. Anticipating my exhaustion, he offered my favorite comforts: a good cup of coffee and flowers.

I'm blessed to have this man in my life. Our relationship, however, is not the result of good luck, but of our applying the principles offered in this book.

The spiritual practice here is that neither of us thinks, "When was the last time you did something for *me*." The spiritual practice is to demonstrate our love through an act of devotion.

The same is true of our relationship with God. We perform certain rituals—such as regular prayer—to connect with our Creator in a deeper, more meaningful way.

~~~~~~~~~

The spiritual practice here is that neither of us thinks, "When was the last time you did something for *me*." The spiritual practice is to demonstrate our love through an act of devotion.

~~~~~~~~~

Many of my Jewish friends affix a mezuzah to the front door-post of their home. A mezuzah is a small box containing a biblical commandment to love and remember God. My friends have a ritual of touching the mezuzah whenever they open or close the door to remind them of God's Presence. You can create an altar space in your home—by doing something as simple as lighting a candle—to show your devotion to God. I have designated a sacred place in my home for prayer. Prayer can happen at any time and in any location, but a special feeling arises when it becomes part of a personal ceremony.

We connect with God in so many ways, from the thoughts we think to the questions we ask. We communicate in a myriad of ways; but it is through ritual that we celebrate the divine relationship.

~~~~~~~~~

Loving rituals help to bring a perfect spiritual love to our imperfect, human relationships.

~~~~~~~~~

Loving rituals help to bring a perfect spiritual love to our imperfect, human relationships. Through them, we design our future. Through them, we place ourselves in a perpetual state of giving. Through them, we rekindle our natural curiosity, asking ourselves, "What act would this person most appreciate?"

Through them, we demonstrate, "What matters to you, matters to me." Through them, we move one step closer to our Creator, who performs the ultimate loving ritual by granting us the gift of life, day after day after day.

Thoughts That Transform

~ Every day brings me a fresh opportunity to demonstrate love. What act will I do today that will create a beautiful memory for someone else?

~ "Do this in remembrance of Me," Jesus said, inviting me into communion. When I perform a loving ritual, I am deepening my relationship with God, the source of all love.

~ Through ritual, I celebrate my loved ones.

Practice

List the rituals you perform for those closest to you. If such traditions are lacking, make a point to establish at least one loving act that you repeat every week. Start simply. Maybe leave work early every Friday to pick up your kids at school and take them out for milk shakes. Perhaps you can arrange a weekly mystery drive.

If you do engage in rituals, ask yourself, "Do these customs reflect what I think is important or what matters most to the other person?" Like Peter, you may be unaware that your efforts are misdirected until the truth literally hits you over the head.

Loving rituals not only benefit others, but deepen and enrich our relationship with ourselves. Think of the customs that comfort. Maybe you enjoy indulging in a hot bath, complete with candlelight and soft music, or like taking walks in the woods. How often have you done those very things lately? Consider giving yourself the gift of a loving ritual.

Establish a ritual to express your love for God. Perhaps you choose to have your first thought of the day be one of gratitude to your Creator. Maybe you decide, no matter how busy or frenetic your day, to take a few minutes and talk over with God what's on your mind. Yes, God is with us regardless, but the ritual allows us to remember that we are with God as well.

Epilogue

In the early thirteenth century, a Sufi mystic named Mevlana Jalaluddin Rumi posed a puzzle to mankind in the form of a poem. He wrote:

> *It is as if a king has sent you to a country to carry out one special, specific task. You go to the country and you perform a hundred other tasks, but if you have not performed the task for which you were sent, it is as if you have performed nothing at all. So man has come into the world for a particular task, and that is his purpose. If he doesn't perform it, he will have done nothing.*

There his words end. For centuries, great thinkers have pondered Rumi's meaning. What is the particular task we are meant to accomplish? What can be of such importance that any other feat we undertake, any acclaim we garner, will be rendered worthless if we ignore this one task?

As we have discovered together through these pages, we are here for the purpose of learning to express perfect love: with God, with ourselves and with others. This divine task, once undertaken, is never completed. In the journey of life, we intersect with some people for the most fleeting moment: the person standing in front of us at the grocery store, the ticket taker at the airport. There are others with whom we travel a great distance.

Whoever these people may be, however much time we spend together, we can practice more perfect loving. By carrying out the king's—our Creator's—mission every day of our lives, we will bring forth the greatness that, deep down, we have always known was our destiny.

Go in love.

ACKNOWLEDGMENTS

This book is important to me because it is about the precious seed of greatness within us all and the possibility of its fruit of perfect love in our everyday lives. I am grateful to all the people who have contributed to my journey of discovery thus far and also those who willingly shared their stories and lessons in these pages.

A special thanks to Christy Scattarella. Without your help in compiling years of sermons, this book would not be written. I deeply appreciate your dedication to this project, your love and care for the message it contains, and your great talent in helping translate my speaking into the written word. You are a true gift.

I also want to thank Rachel Duvack, Chris Adams, and Ginger Hendricks. Your help with the research for this project as well as your ongoing support and belief for its outcome means more to me than you know.

A heartfelt gratitude to my editor, Toni Burbank. Your support, encouragement, and call to really give the reader something not only inspirational but authentically useful has made this book not only better but something I am truly proud of. Thank you, Toni.

A special thanks to my prayer partners, Rev. Wendy Craig Purcell, Rev. Richard Rogers, Rev. Howard Caesar, and Scott Benge. Your faith has real power and many a time over the last two years, it was your support that gave new life and energy to this project. I appreciate and love each of you.

I am deeply grateful for the faith and support of my friends, Sue Gilbert, Rhonda Siegrist, and John and Sally Benn. You have made a quantum difference.

Particular thanks to my dynamic women's group, aka "The G.G.'s," Rev. Faith Moran, Debbie Tallman, and Colleen Schuerlein. You are a powerful trio of supporters and believers. I am grateful to God for each one of you.

To my sister Jackie, thank you for encouraging me, loving me, and believing in me. I am blessed beyond words that we are sisters and we are friends.

To my parents, Jack and Dorothy Manin: Thank you, Mom and Dad. Your sixty-plus-year marriage is one of the great love stories. Your ability and willingness to be exceptional parents has framed my life. I am blessed to have seen and known your beautiful example.

To my children, John, Richard, Jennifer, Mat, Michael, and Matthew: Thank you for the opportunity to be your mom, to learn from you and together to grow in love. You, your spouses—Dora, Kelli and Jorge—as well as your children—Ricardo, Allie, Kayla, Kiara, and Braden—are all great beings and tremendous blessings.

And especially to Ed, my husband, beloved partner, soul mate, colleague, and best friend: Thank you for your support, guidance, and daily encouragement, not only for this book but for the deeply held dream of the message it contains. In your faith, I have taken steps I didn't know I could. In your challenge to go deeper, I have found so much more to me than I knew before. In your love, I have experienced the promise of what I always believed was possible between a man and a woman.

ABOUT THE AUTHOR

An ordained minister since 1975, MARY MANIN MORRISSEY is the founder and senior minister of the Living Enrichment Center in Wilsonville, Oregon, which serves 4,000 people weekly. Her previous book, *Building Your Field of Dreams,* was adapted for a one-hour PBS special. She has addressed the United Nations on curbing violence, worked with the Dalai Lama on interfaith dialogue, and received countless humanitarian awards.